Skullduggery

Skullduggery

Kerry O'Keeffe

Cartoons by Boo Bailey

ABC
Books

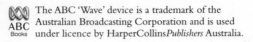 The ABC 'Wave' device is a trademark of the Australian Broadcasting Corporation and is used under licence by HarperCollinsPublishers Australia.

This edition comprised of selected columns written by Kerry O'Keeffe for the *Sunday Telegraph*, plus selected stories from *According to Skull* (ABC Books, 2004) and *Turn Turn Turn ... Please!* (ABC Books, 2007), as well as previously unpublished material.

This collection published in Australia in 2010
by HarperCollinsPublishers Australia Pty Limited
ABN 36 009 913 517
harpercollins.com.au

HarperCollinsPublishers
25 Ryde Road, Pymble, Sydney, NSW 2073, Australia
31 View Road, Glenfield, Auckland 0627, New Zealand
A 53, Sector 57, Noida, UP, India
77–85 Fulham Palace Road, London W6 8JB, United Kingdom
2 Bloor Street East, 20th floor, Toronto, Ontario M4W 1A8, Canada
10 East 53rd Street, New York NY 10022, USA

National Library of Australia Cataloguing-in-Publication entry:

O'Keeffe, Kerry, 1949-
Skullduggery / Kerry O'Keeffe.
978 0 7333 2596 0 (pbk.)
Cricket — Anecdotes.
Other Authors/Contributors: Australian Broadcasting Corporation.
796.358

Cover photograph of Kerry O'Keeffe by Steve Baccon
Cover design by Matt Stanton
Internal design by Alicia Freile, Tango Media
Typeset in 11/19pt Minion Pro by Kirby Jones
Printed and bound in Australia by Griffin Press
70gsm Classic used by HarperCollinsPublishers is a natural, recyclable product made from wood grown in sustainable forests. The manufacturing processes conform to the environmental regulations in the country of origin, Finland.

6 5 4 3 2 1   10 11 12 13 14

Contents

Skullduggery

Spotting the Fix

It was a typical night after yet another day of appalling golf. Melancholic, contemplating lawn bowls, I was sitting wistfully on the couch watching England and Pakistan go hard at each other. Or so I thought. My 20-year-old son looked subdued beside me … what was he doing here? He doesn't even play golf! Mohammed Amir was making the ball behave more erratically than Lindsay Lohan. At once I announced that this lad would make millions out of the game – I didn't factor in the recent allegations of spot-fixing.

On the screen the cricket was tough, trying-for-your-life stuff. The England number three, Jonathan Trott, an obsessive-compulsive South African who has unmistakeably cloned his demeanour and shot-making on Steve Waugh, was giving a masterclass in how to counter skilful swing bowling. He is the key to the Poms retaining the urn this summer. Trott requests his guard at least once an over – sometimes twice. In his lifetime, Douglas Bader would have asked for fewer leg stumps.

Then came 'that' no-ball from Amir. This was no-slip on a greasy approach despite the fact sawdust was promptly ordered. It looked a far-from-subtle deliberate overstepping. Kyle Sandilands couldn't have crossed the line by a bigger distance. Teenagers can be mediocre at sleight of hand or foot. Curiously, the delivery itself was not particularly spiteful – there seemed to be no wild-eyed intention to crib closer for a body strike. Amir hadn't seen red … he may have simply been chasing 'green'!

I was at a loss to explain to my son how the Pakistani paceman could get it so wrong. The side-on replay was damning – oddly, however, not as much for Amir as for the fieldsman supposedly moving in with the bowler at short extra-cover. One single frame (which I have now forensically watched dozens of times) said a great deal. The captain, Salman Butt, was that man at short extra-cover … every fielder in this position must be watching the batsman at the moment the ball is released. He is duty bound to focus on the striker. Not Salman Butt: his eyes were only for the illegal front foot of Amir … his sight was firmly set on where the bowler's right boot had landed. Was an order about to be carried out? And yes … a huge no-ball! Ka-ching, ka-ching? We won't know until the ICC hands down its findings.

And yes, it was the first delivery of the third over – just as that scallywag in the hoodie had predicted on the *News of the World* footage. Seriously, that guy needs fashion advice – if you're counting out 150,000 quid and trying desperately to impress a potential client, a designer label suit may have sealed the deal ... but a hoodie? Of course, all of this could be a massive co-incidence. Whatever the outcome of the ICC investigation, which, on disclosed form, we should know by Princess Mary's twins' 21st birthday, there are bound to be victims.

The 18-year-old wunderkind Amir could well be mourned. Adolescents in cricket are much influenced by their seniors. When I first entered the Australian test team in the early '70s, the elder statesmen set a moustache and mullet standard. I shunned both – you have to take a stand on some things. Mohammed Amir must wish the allegations against him were only about his bogan hairstyle. Mohammed Asif, a brilliant trundler with an eye for trouble that the Baldwin brothers would admire, is again under the kosh. And then there is Butt – an intelligent, highly respected leader of his country's cricket team – who should have been watching the batsman on strike!

And there is still that recurring image of the alleged fixer boasting of how fat the odds of 40/1 had been about Australia coming from behind to beat the Pakistanis in the Sydney Test last

January. I called that game for ABC Radio. During the visitors'
absurd, scatter-brained and eventually unsuccessful run chase on
that fourth afternoon, I was having coffee with a reputable Irish
journalist on his way to cover the Under-19 World Cup in New
Zealand. After a clutter of wickets, there were two or three overs
of intelligent, risk-free run gathering.

'They're not playing according to the script,' quipped 'Paddy'.

'Oh, you cynical thing,' I fired back before disdainfully
moving away.

Sadly, even cynics sometimes get it right.

5 September 2010

On My Selection

The Mentalist would find it difficult to fathom what has been going on in the heads of the Australian selection panel over the past few weeks. Fair dinkum, was the current spin-bowling order of merit conceived at Hooters during a session with John Daly?

Last Wednesday the Aussies began a crucial test in Delhi needing to take 20 wickets to level the series. Our panel came up with the slow-bowling trio of Cameron White, Michael Clarke and Simon Katich. Despite their genuine cricket talent, this grouping is unlikely to take 20 first-class wickets in a calendar year on doctored decks in the Gobi Desert. Is Jason Krejza sleeping inside the Taj Mahal with Stuart MacGill's alarm clock?

And why is baby-faced Chinaman Beau Casson now considered fruit out of season? Casson's situation demands a public explanation from chairman Hilditch, whom the media feel is harder to catch than the multiple top edges he provided at fine leg during his hooking days. Come on, 'Digger', feed the chooks some crumbs! Casson's case is particularly perplexing: the New South Welshman contributed in his only test in the West Indies last June but has been overlooked for the subcontinent series. Rumour abounds that the panel felt a couple of hidings from Sachin Tendulkar and the boys may have torpedoed the slow bowler's career ... and that they were uncomfortable sending two wrist spinners in Bryce McGain and Casson on the same assignment. Chaps, the rule should be to send your best bowlers on difficult missions!

Of course, Casson may not be the real deal anyway ... like Brad Hogg, his wrong 'un is a much stronger delivery than his stock ball and, consequently, represents his major strike option. With Shane Warne and MacGill, the stock ball was forever their genuine wicket-taker. And Casson, too, has to develop his momentum on slow pitches where batsmen tend to play him a little too comfortably off the back foot. These are challenges Beau has been denied by selection panel perceptions. Perhaps, however, Casson's googlies will return against New Zealand this month in Australia – the Kiwis would have trouble picking Bill Lawry's nose!

The Casson issue aside, surely the off spinner Krejza had to play in this Delhi test. Ricky Ponting is known to be a fan and could have cuddled the former New South Welshman had the going got tough at Feroz Shah Kotla. Part-time offie Virender Sehwag claimed three vital wickets on the third day to prove how valuable finger spin can be on such crusty surfaces. This was Krejza's pitch, too!

Having said that, Nathan Hauritz, the New South Wales off spinner, was the best finger spinner I saw last season – although I didn't take in Greg Matthews of Sydney University. 'Haurie' ticks the two most important boxes in the art of slow bowling: he possesses a genuine loop and he's precise – two skills we've sadly lacked in India of late. Hauritz is a far better bowler today than when he was last in India in 2004. The shoulder injury to McGain has sparked a chain of irrational selections … add Simon Baker to the national panel and allow psychic reason to rule!

Retiring Cricket Australia chairman Creagh O'Connor lamented recently that Indigenous and European cricketers have not surfaced during his tenure. Don't worry, Creagh, exciting youngsters with exotic surnames are at hand. Here are three whom I feel will gain international honours within the next three years:

Usman Khawaja (NSW)

Born in Pakistan, this prodigiously talented left-handed opener could be our first Muslim test cap! Khawaja and Macksville star Phillip Hughes could well be the opening combination when England come to Australia in 2011. There is the small matter of the marvellous Shaun Marsh, but his footwork and stand-and-deliver outlook may be better suited in the middle order. If Khawaja was a race horse his breeding would read: by Gautam Gambhir out of Mark Taylor. The 21-year-old possesses the wide stroke range of Gambhir but also has that 'Tubby' trait of not getting out when he's 'in'!

Moisés Henriques (NSW)

The St George all rounder was born in Portugal and has had to spell his name on registration days more often than Fuifui Moimoi. Henriques is a middle-order batsman first and a bowler second. His short career has already been punctuated by long periods of injury: this strapping all rounder could strain a groin salting chips! Fit and in form Henriques will challenge Andrew Symonds and Shane Watson in the years ahead.

Theo Doropoulos (WA)

I can't recall a Greek in the Australian team – Lenny Pascoe (né Durtanovich) was a mix of everything – but Theo is primarily a 'bubble and squeak'! This 23-year-old played such a crunching high quality on-drive for six in a recent one-day match that it reeked higher honours … to me, anyway. If he resists the temptation to change his name to Ted Poole, a one-day cap could arrive within two years for this confident stroke maker.

2 November 2008

Our Adoring Public

The Australian sports public has concluded that Muttiah Muralitharan continues to chuck, Bart Cummings is a freak and Andrew Symonds should be returned immediately to the Test cricket team.

Murali could have his right elbow fused so it is straighter than Fred Nile yet consistently propel viper-like off spinners and the mob would still scream 'no ball'! Cummings may be simply a hard-working octogenarian with a knack for getting horses to stay longer than an annoying mother-in-law … unanimously, though, his gift is seen as freakish. His eyebrows, however, are a matter of public concern. Legislation should be passed to have Bart's brows back-burnt. With the bushfire season at hand, a stray match on a hot day and that facial forest could incinerate Sydney!

And then there is 'Roy' … still in the naughty corner while Ricky Ponting's team may be handing back the Border-Gavaskar Trophy in India. Axed because he went fishing and necked some 'frothies' the day before taking on Bangladesh, Symonds remains in exile. In the '70s, that sort of behaviour was called … touring! Fair dinkum, you could charter a boat and demolish a keg of beer during the lunch break against the Bangers and still flog them by 100 or so runs by six o'clock. Punters think Symonds has done his time and should be allowed back into the fold.

Indeed, he would have been handy in Delhi last week after Gautam Ghambir stuck an elbow into Shane Watson … 'Roy' could have sorted out the 'Gaut', I'm sure. His shouldering of the poor streaker at the Gabba last summer remains the best shirt front on a cricket field ever, I reckon … though Rugby League hard man Malcolm Reilly, had he switched codes, could have brought a new meaning to elbowing the bowler. The Englishman's victims normally couldn't eat fairy floss for six weeks!

But I digress. Huge numbers of Aussie supporters lament Symonds' absence from the current series: 'We've missed a match winner,' they chorused. Well, at his best and test cricket hungry … yes! But 'Roy', sadly, is far from the pinkest of form. His restoration to Ponting's team should be dependent on Sheffield Shield runs and wickets … to recall him against New Zealand at the Gabba later this month without any substantial performance would be a gamble. Questions have to be asked and answered. Is 'Roy' still genuinely in love with Test cricket? Despite his extreme wealth through the IPL contract and his endorsements, does he retain the hunger of a Michael Hussey? And are his off spinners as effective as they were prior to his shoulder operation? The man in the street would have him back in a heartbeat. Their contention is that Symonds is an intimidator whom opponents fear. Streakers, too, tend to rug up when he's around. The public want him at the Gabba on November 20 … we'll find out the mood of the selectors and senior players soon enough.

Attention all high school science teachers out there. Tired of having your sinks burnt? Uncomfortable with hydrochloric acid being thrown at you every second week? Here is an opportunity to join an elite sporting team badly in need of a nerd. If your knowledge of scientific experiments extends to changing the direction of a cricket ball flight, please apply at once to Mr Tim Nielsen, c/- Australian Cricket Team. The Troy Cooleys have done a pretty reasonable job but this requires a white-coated professor. Our bowlers – particularly the quick men and the very impressive Jason Krejza – need a scientist to teach them how to apply the laws of physics in regard to propelling a leather sphere. The Aussie pacemen in India have not shown the same reverse swing skills of their opponents, and Krejza is all bounce and over spin. Despite his exceptional eight-wicket performance debut in Nagpur, the Tasmanian off spinner will add another dimension to his finger spin if he learns how to curve the rock. With the Ashes in England just around the corner we have to foster skilful reverse swingers and curve spinners. Is Julius Sumner Miller still alive? Where is Brother Marcellin from the 1967 Marist Kogarah Year 12 Science Department? Aussie cricket is seeking a geek!

8 November 2008

A Little Less Conversation ...

Has there ever been a greater overreaction to a couple of bowling changes? Sorry, people, but India already had a winning score by tea on day four in Nagpur. Dennis Lillee and Charlie 'Terror' Turner – great strike men – could not have affected the result after those twenty minutes of scones and jam. On sandy surfaces, Ricky Ponting may not be Rommel but he is definitely not Thomas Blamey, either. 'Punter's great sin is that he wastes too much time talking to his trundlers before an over starts. Our skipper covers everything in his two-minute chats to bowlers: chef Matt Hayden's far-too-crispy crackling the night before ... the prospects of the red box in the fourth at Wentworth Park later than evening. Fair dinkum, most bowlers – particularly the quick men – have the attention span of Homer Simpson: they've forgotten instructions by the third erotic rub of the ball on their groin.

Ian Chappell, a blunt skipper, only ever said two things to me when I had the ball in my hand: 'Have a rest, Skull' or 'Are you happy with the field?' To the letter, if I said yes – which I normally did – play proceeded immediately. Privately I yearned to ask for three more fieldsmen but I figured it might have sent the wrong message.

Ponting is a victim of trying to tactically conjure wickets with a bowling attack that frequently proved more expensive than a ticket to watch Andre Rieu fiddle! And then the gobbledegook behind the rationale that Cameron White was the bowler of choice to dismiss Harbhajan Singh. Frankly, in his current form 'Whitey' couldn't get a bindi-eye out of a heel with gelignite! Sure, 'Punter' may have got it wrong, but India had the Test sewn up anyway. Let's move on … thank God for New Zealand!

Normal Test transmission will be resumed on Thursday at 'fortress Gabba', back on pitches where the ball comes onto the bat, stung by criticism, 'Roy' in front of the faithful and a New Zealand outfit without traditional Christian names like Blair or Bevan.

This could be a three-day Test. Without Shane Warne, Glen McGrath and Adam Gilchrist, Test matches are lasting five days – player's golf handicaps are suffering! 'Punter' could soon be out to three if the situation is not arrested. It should be this week. The Black Caps have an unestablished opening batting pair and an unsettled new ball attack ... opponents who lack both combinations are generally obliterated on Australian pitches. There are some positive signs, nonetheless. Daniel Vettori is possibly bowling better than at any stage of his career: his drifting left arm spinners are swinging more than Elton John. With the cue, the Kiwis will introduce a fatty-boomstick number three who has yet to knock back an offer to upsize. Good onya, Jesse Ryder!

All the mail from an off-season international 'A' team tournament in Darwin was that J. Ryder was the best batsman on show. And he's got form off the field: suspension for alcohol-related incidents and his frustration with the constant surveillance of his waistline make Jesse a person of interest. Laid low by a virus this weekend, Vettori will be desperate for the big-hitting left hander to be whacking it over mid-wicket next weekend in Brisbane. And watch out too for Chris Martin, their strike fast bowler. This fellow is not Ishant Sharma but he gets plenty of bounce, hits the seam and already has a five-wicket haul at the Gabba on a previous visit. Martin, too, has a stranglehold on the title of worst batsman in world cricket: currently averaging a paltry 2.38 runs per Test innings, 'Marto' makes Glen McGrath look like Sachin Tendulkar. And, to boot, the Black Cap number eleven is considered more capable with the stick at Test level than the short forms ... in twenty one-day internationals his batting average stands at 1.60 per innings. Someone find me a ball!

16 November 2008

Walters Sets Sydney-London Record

As the 1977 Australian Ashes cricket squad boarded the Qantas Boeing on that balmy April afternoon, there was the usual amount of excitement and anticipation in the group. Some players were meeting each other as team-mates for the first time ... and England was the tour so many of us had always coveted. There was nibblies and a few drinks prior to departure from Mascot Airport ... family and friends were farewelled ... and the jet bound for Heathrow was suddenly in the air.

Within a short time what had begun as a bonding couple of drinks turned into quite an event ... it was pondered by a senior player: 'I wonder how many beers someone could sink between now and London?' Dangerous question with the calibre of imbiber in this party, I mused at the time. Almost at once a contest was struck … rules were simple … a drinker would receive one point for every can of beer downed – to ensure there was no cheating, the drinker had to shake the can so the recorders could hear noise of the ring top at the bottom on the container. Two points would be allocated for a spirit. Hell, I thought … if one of our squad can drink spirits for 22 hours we either have a very special team-mate or someone with a problem. If the competition itself appeared unrefined, the score sheet was even cruder – a sickness bag … unused, at that stage.

I sat there, cradling my second or third beer, and reflected on a betting marked for this marathon. This is a fair summation of the field:

Doug Walters (NSW)	5–2
Rod Marsh (WA)	3–1
Mick Malone (WA)	5–1
Ray Bright (VIC)	6–1
Gary Cosier (SA)	8–1
Kerry O'Keeffe (NSW)	10–1
Geoff Dymock (QLD)	12–1
Jeff Thomson (QLD)	16–1
The Rest	5000–1

Let's look at the form guide.

Doug Walters: 5–2 Entitled to favouritism. Has undeniable results over long distances. Trained to the minute. A real stayer ... will be hard to run down over the final stages. Possibly has two livers!!

Rod Marsh: 3–1 Proven over the course. He and Walters might cut at each other out in front, however, and be vulnerable to a swooper. Possesses billiard table legs that are capable of holding litres for long periods. Genuine threat to the favourite if he can pace himself. Very tough down the straight.

Mick Malone: 5–1 Reported to have tremendous form around Perth. Fellow Western Australian Marsh regards him as a huge threat. Did a lot of his trackwork at the Scarborough Social Club and a number of his drinking group reckon he can handle the step up in class. Watch the market ... he's the sly tip to knock out the topweights.

Ray Bright: 6–1 Cut his teeth on the 1974 Australian tour of New Zealand ... Impressed keen judges like Ian Chappell with his willingness to mix it in Group One company. Coming off a very solid preparation during the 1977 New Zealand tour under the seasoned manager Roger Wotten of Gunnedah. Will give a good account of himself but may find the pace unsuitable. Can stay all day, nonetheless.

Gary Cosier: 8–1 Very good weight-for-age campaigner. Another from the Ian Chappell stable who will race forward. Unknown over the distance but may give cheek for a long time.

Kerry O'Keeffe: 10–1 Capable of causing an upset on his day. Been well prepared by mentor Graeme Langlands, a Rugby League Immortal. Slow starter but has powerful finish … if the front markers hit the wall, he may storm down outside and get the money. Check out his left eye … if it starts to close, he's no chance.

Geoff Dymock: 12–1 Has reasonable form on Queensland tracks. A quiet sipper who will be there or thereabouts all the way. The mail is that when he hits the wall, he gibbers. Watch for repetition of the same sentence.

Jeff Thomson: 16–1 Outstanding social drinker. Possibly not a contender here because unlike a few of the favourites, he knows when he's had enough. If he feels in control, he's worth an each way bet. If he can't get the journey in his own mind, he won't complete the course. Possibly too sensible to be the winner.

With the market established and form guide fully analysed, it was down to business. One of the extreme outsiders – Kim Hughes – was an early leader ... he burst out of the gates ... talking a big race ... and drinking spirits (worth two points). Nobody thought he'd last ... as the plane flew across the Queensland border he'd cleared out with 12 points. Two hours out of Darwin all of it was on the aisle floor!!! His campaign was over.

By Singapore, the favourites had the race to themselves. Half the field had already retired ... Lenny Pascoe, a fiery fast bowler with a balanced view on behaviour, was an early exit. Craig Sargeant, a cultured pharmacist from Perth looked somewhat perplexed by an end-of-tour ritual being conducted pre-tour. What the heck ... we're off to England. Marsh and Walters were already setting a cracking pace ... Malone was making his presence felt ... Bright, predictably, was just behind the leading group. I was nicely placed, flanked by Cosier and Dymock, and comfortable in the going.

The hours ground on ... there were more and more casualties ... soon it was obvious that Walters and Marsh would have it to themselves. Thirty five beers each just out of Bahrain!!! My left eye is starting to close … but I'm a chance for a podium finish … third in this company would be quite a performance. The sickness bag doubling as a scorecard is looking decidedly soggy.

We're inside Bahrain Airport … in the transit lounge … Walters looks in reasonable shape … playing cards with anybody who will sit next to him. How dehydrated must he be … thirty odd cans of beer … and he's smoked at least fifty cigarettes. This guy is a machine.

How's 'Bacchus' Marsh? Not travelling as well as Walters and he's one can behind him. Another surefire sign he's feeling the pinch is that every robe-clad Arab he bumps into, he mumbles 'I'm sorry, Lawrence!'

It's been a long flight … we're over the twenty hour mark … and Heathrow Airport is not far away. I've called off the jam and will leave it to the judges to decide if I am to be awarded third place. The leaders, Walters and Marsh, will definitely fight out the finish … they look shabby … Marsh has fallen asleep and there is phlegm making its way down his chin. Walters is attempting to light the filter of his sixtieth cigarette for the journey.

Suddenly we're touching down … the judges are tallying the ticks on the air sickness bag … we have a winner – Doug Walters with 44 cans is declared our champion!! Marsh is second with 43 – and subsequently declares he'll better that next time

he flys to London. Third is contentious because the scoresheet has disintegrated into a soggy mess of tissue. I claim the bronze medal but protests are fired in immediately. Walters, though, has justified his favouritism with an all-the-way victory. He proudly leads us off the plane to a batallion of Fleet Street press hungry for a headline. 'Aussies on Drinking Binge' would have been their lead story … we covered our tracks reasonably well, however. Marsh did in fact go on to establish a new mark of 45 cans a few years later ... and was escorted off the plane in a wheelchair on that occasion.

Pundits thought that record would stand for a long time but along came that Launceston bull dog, David Boon ... he posted 53 cans on his flight ... a new mark which will probably last forever!!

Still, it was great to be a part of that initial trail blazing 'bender' ... I guess??!!

The Big Man of Cricket

If Long John Daly played cricket he'd choose to live in the body of Jesse Ryder. I've never met big Jesse … but I just love the star Kiwi fatty boomstick. This fellow is an elite sportsman who looks as if he's never volunteered to be the designated driver for a night on the town. A bloke who, hovering over a huge plate of pavlova, has never uttered, 'Oh, I shouldn't'. Jesse has a genuine crack! Despite suspending him for alcohol-related incidents, New Zealand Cricket cannot ignore the big guy, basically because he's just too good. After Jesse put his hand through a glass window at 4 am the other year, he had to endure a spell on the sidelines. Anyone can put their hand through a glass window at that time. It's normally pretty dark!

I carry weight myself ... why? Because I happen to like eating and drinking. What a sinner I am! Though I do not consider myself obese, one in two men I meet seem to feel a somewhat red-blooded urge to pat my stomach and utter something banal like 'Puttin' on a bit, Skull' or 'You've been in a good paddock, mate!' Inane opening lines are a particular hobby horse of mine. If I bump into someone who has added 60 kilos since our last meeting I generally open with, 'I like what you've done with your hair'. I mean you wouldn't walk up to John Wayne Bobbitt and say 'How's it hanging?' I reckon conversations should start as positively as possible. I don't care if Jesse Ryder is seen as being five pick handles across the backside. Jesse is a flag bearer. He gives hope to pears; he has shown aspiring youngsters that you can bat number three for your country without the body fat levels of Nicole Ritchie. He has proven that should clipboard-wielding nerds be forced to measure your skin folds with barbeque tongs then that's okay! Runs and wickets should be the only measuring stick ... not callipers.

And there have been other fatsos before big Jesse. Queensland's Greg 'Fat Cat' Ritchie was a superb striker of the ball who fought ongoing battles with spectators and media about his girth. More than once 'Cat' angrily accused newspaper photographers of deliberately trying to snap him at his unflattering worst. Arjuna

Ranatunga should have been more respected for his batting talents and refusal to give ground to Australians. Instead the portly Sri Lankan captain became the figure of scorn. He was once cruelly refused a runner by an Australian skipper because he was 'fat and unfit'. During a tight Test match in Sydney, Ian Healy used Arjuna's love of a feed in a clever sledge. Before the Sri Lankan was to face up to a Shane Warne over, Healy loudly suggested to David Boone at short leg: 'Hey, Boonie, I reckon we can get this fatty stumped ... Put a Mars Bar just short of a good length, that's sure to get him out of his crease!' Harsh and unfair. Then there was the very frustrated fast bowler who asked Zimbabwean pig

farmer Edo Brandes after he played and missed a few times, 'Why are you so fat?' Brandes quipped back, 'Because every time I make love to your wife, she gives me a biscuit.' Ouch! And of course there is Inzamam-Ul-Huq, a great but slow-moving Pakistani batsman who has been run out more than Dennis Ferguson.

The South Australian Redback selectors do not seem to know what to do with strapping – no, make that portly – batsman Mark 'Cossie' Cosgrove. Such a gifted strokemaker, Cossie was earmarked for a long international career not so long ago but his playing time has been limited by enforced time on the sidelines for being six doughnuts over par. The unanimously popular Darren Lehmann liked a beer, a smoke and carbohydrates, butbecause 'Boof' succeeded so often on the field his shape escaped undue scrutiny. The message is clear in cricket: if your body compares favourably with Meatloaf, don't fail!

Jesse Ryder managed a couple of wickets and a competent 30 in his first innings at the Gabba. I don't care that the big bloke moves his feet about as quickly as Douglas Bader. Just as John Daly is my favourite golfer, Ryder is my favourite international cricketer this summer ... just for being there!

23 November 2008

Lovable Larrikins

Though I've never been on a night out with Andrew Symonds, it appears you would get in less trouble spending a Mad Monday with Oasis. Frankly, Symonds looks desperately in need of a mentor: not a life coach … a drinking coach! While I'm not saying 'Roy' is a two-pot screamer, it is common knowledge around the Aussie camp that the burly all rounder has a low tolerance for alcohol.

Enter Darren 'Boof' Lehmann – a man who hour after hour could neck amber fluid strained through John Daly's golf glove and retain his dignity. Cricket Australia should immediately appoint 'Boof' as Symonds' beer bitch. The Queenslander already has a healthy respect for the former left hander's capacity. Back in 2005, on the day of that ill-fated match against Bangladesh in Cardiff, Symonds rang Lehmann at 5 am to invite him for a few jars.

If you want advice on marriage, you ring 'Warney', should you need help with a binding contract 'Chock' Mundine is your man, but the go-to guy for a drink before sunrise just has to be 'Boof'! Given that 'Roy' has publicly stated he's not going on the wagon, he has to learn to make clear-headed decisions in licensed premises.

My era was lucky: media scrutiny of off-field misbehaviour was as intense as coverage of inter-club croquet. Humungous drinking sessions in the '70s went unreported basically because print journalists were part of the benders!

But there always seemed to be a certain decorum. Dougie Walters drank in hundreds of half-star hotels where grizzled pensioners would sidle up and offer boorish advice on how he should play the hook shot. All were listened to and bought beers until they were incapable of operating their Zimmer frames. Young punks, from the other side of the bar, would one minute scream out, 'You're an overrated hoax, Walters,' and the next minute be bludging a cigarette off him. Doug never held a grudge beyond the next mouthful. As Walters proved, the public will embrace a sports hero who can handle his squirt.

The very mention of David Boon to most Australians will draw a smile and an accompanying groan of 'legend'. Throughout his whole career the little Tasmanian tippled away at bars without incident – nobody cared that he may have had the conversation versatility of Lurch – you were on the drink with Boonie. 'Roy', too, likes getting out at night – it's no sin – unlike Mike Hussey, who said recently that in the daily plan that rules his life he goes to bed religiously at 9.30 pm and never drinks coffee in the afternoon. Note to self ... avoid 'Mr Cricket' when holidaying!

Then there was Shane Warne – the man who chooses Midori over beer and who himself frequents the odd nightclub. Nonetheless, never in Warney's long and much celebrated career have I spoken to anybody who claims to have seen the leg-spinning legend the worse for liquor. It's a shock, I know, but fact.

Despite his own history of trouble, Australia wants to love big 'Roy': when Ricky Ponting brought him into the attack against New Zealand on Friday in Adelaide, the crowd erupted in prolonged applause. 'Roy', however, has to learn to embrace the public. The culture seems to have developed in the Australian squad where well-wishers are classified as 'niff nuffs'. In retirement, as I have found out, the current players will discover that these 'nuffies' have generally achieved and led far more interesting lives than themselves. With 'Boof's expertise Symonds can lift his game ... and then maybe come out unscathed after a couple with Oasis.

30 November 2008

Dale Pales in Comparison

Sorry to be a stick in the mud, but the rave notices that I've been hearing and reading about South African boom paceman Dale Steyn have been completely over the top. Marcia Hines could not have painted a more glowing picture of this fellow's unlimited potential to wreak havoc this summer … well here comes awful realist Kyle!

Steyn has, indeed, had a great twelve months … knocking over chumps! Who would have thought that fast outswingers might destroy the might of New Zealand and Bangladesh? My wife – a canny, dibbly dobbly trundler whose only cricket outing comes each Christmas Day in the carport – could sneak one past Kiwi Chris Martin's defence. I'm not saying he's the worst batsman of all time but when the Black Cap number eleven walked out to bat on the last day of the Adelaide Test, he strolled past the after-match presentation dais where Mark Taylor was already conducting an interview with Dan Vettori!

Of course, Steyn can only play what's in front of him, and the paceman has dined out on the Kiwis and Bangladeshis in recent times. The next month, however, against Ricky Ponting's crack squad, will determine whether his ranking as the number one bowler in Test cricket is genuine. I watched Steyn strut his stuff on cable television against England during our winter … and, yes, he can bowl 'jaffas', but old 'Warney' would love the prolific number of 'pies' he serves up at the same time. Steyn needs swinging conditions to be a real factor!

Against the Poms, the right handers – particularly Kevin 'Pumpkin Head' Pietersen repeatedly whipped the South African quick man through mid-wicket from the line of leg stump. Australia has consummate leg side players like Ponting and Michael Clarke who will feast on non-swinging half-volleys on their pads. And the left-handed trio of Matthew Hayden, Simon Katich and Mike Hussey are meaner than Nurse Ratched when it comes to dispatching poorly directed inswingers through square leg.

From my observation, Steyn's best work is done when he is fresh – his form fell away towards the end of the English tour. The

Perth Test will be his best opportunity to confirm his reputation but I can't see him living up to the hype.

Steyn's partner, Morné Morkel, may be a more difficult proposition on bouncy pitches however, the 6 foot 6 giant has a history of no-balling that would make a eunuch flinch!

If the umpires ping him for every over-stepping, Morkel may struggle for consistency. Against the Poms, the South African paceman offered far too much width to batsmen when under pressure – bowl wide to the Aussie top six at your peril! Morkel is a Courtney Walsh clone with an extra yard of pace. Without no-ball stress and a disciplined line, he could be more effective than Steyn throughout the three tests.

On the other hand, the Proteas' batting looks the real deal: it is now a top six second only to Ponting's men in world rankings. For skipper Graeme Smith this is his biggest challenge – to beat Australia in their own backyard. Note to 'Smithy': Brett Lee has not lost his in-swinger and he has made a living from getting you out lbw!

Neil McKenzie, however, is a much improved opening batsman – this bloke is a trump despite obsessive compulsive behaviour that has seen him run off the field on occasions to check that all the toilet seats in the dressing room are down. Hashim Amla, Jacques Kallis, Ashwell Prince and AB de Villiers is a quartet that can take the South Africans to some big totals if conditions suit.

I am backing the left-handed Prince to be the leading run scorer in the series … cop a tip from Uncle Skull: if you want to beat the deepening recession next year, take whatever odds are available about Ashwell Prince topping the batting aggregate for both teams. Once upon a time 'Warney' could get the inexperienced Prince out with a soggy tomato – the great leg spinner nailed him nine times in eleven Tests. With Warne at the poker table, however, Prince has the wide stroke range, particularly through the cover area, to score heavily against the Australians.

With Steyn not a factor and the psychological scars from previous campaigns still raw, South Africa may not win a test.

Regards, Kyle!

7 December 2008

How to Climb the Cricket Ladder in Six Easy to Follow Steps

Number One – BE TALENTED or make yourself talented

This is the most basic ingredient, of course. You must be either very good mechanically or have your own way of effectiveness. With the latter, if it is technically unsound, you will hit the big hurdles at some stage. Hand–eye co-ordination is a huge factor – you need it in spades.

Batsmen should have at least two very hurtful strokes … be strong off both front and back foot … and not get their stumps hit very much. You cannot have the reputation of 'not being able to hit it off the square' or of 'playing for too many not outs' ... translated these mean you must hit the ball very hard and be prepared to throw your wicket away selflessly in the quest for quicker runs. Batsmen must also be very brave ... the slightest hint that you do not get into line to play faster bowling will give opponents a psychological and physical advantage. Batsmen should be experienced at making big scores from an early age ... once you're on top of the bowlers, you should only rarely ever get yourself out. Tall batsmen must be able to square cut ... thrash the ball through extra cover off the front foot ... and whip it high over mid-on or mid-wicket when the whim takes you. Smaller men must also be prolific square cutters ... clinical cover drivers ... neat through square leg ... and the most productive of on-drives off the front foot. In fact, if your two best strokes are the square cut and the on-drive, you'll get bucketloads of runs whenever you play!! Allan Border had a simple philosophy ... when he practised batting in the nets, he rehearsed not losing his wicket. 'A.B.' would defend the good balls and work a square cut, cover drive or judicious sweep against the others. Such an overview netted him many thousands of Test match runs. Of course, the game is more physical today ... young batsmen practise aggressively. Through my involvement with the New South Wales Emerging

Blues programmes I have seen a great number of teenage batsmen fine tuning their skills in net situations over the last few years. It is not so much that too many of them are using bats so heavy that Dean Lukin, in his prime, would have trouble clean and jerking. Bat weight apart, under-age batsmen practise striking boundaries ... they seem unconcerned about the number of times they are actually dismissed. They strut out of the net having hit 25 boundaries and found a way of getting out five or six times. Asked how they batted, the inevitable reply is 'I "smoked" them!!!' Fair dinkum, it drives me mad. No one seems to ever say I 'worked on a few things' ... a majority just swagger around, happy in the false knowledge that they 'smoked 'em'. These same players get caught at long-on for 10 on Saturday and rationalise the failure with 'I just didn't get enough on it' ... call me a dinosaur, but if you're falling to catches on the long-on fence for under twenty, you're doing more wrong than 'not getting enough on it'.

Bowlers must deliver 'heavy balls' ... they should be taking traditional wickets. By traditional wickets, I mean getting batsmen out according to their craft. Outswing bowlers should be finding or missing the outside edge of batsmen. Inswing bowlers should be opening up a gap between bat and pad and going through it and regularly striking batsmen on the pads. Leg spinners must be defeating the right handers outside edge or inducing snicks to first slip. Off spinners, as with inswingers, have to be frequently going through a right hander's gate or forcing 'lefties' to miss or snick. Nothing else matters other than your stock ball … don't be seen to have a great bouncer or a brilliant wrong-un, if your reputation is not built around the worth of your 'bread and butter' delivery, you're limited!

Wicket-keepers must develop their batting to such an extent that there is occasional speculation about them playing as a specialist batsman. The day of the brilliant gloveman who bats at number ten or eleven is long gone … 'keepers can no longer, either, be seen as even 'he's no mug with the bat' – this is a euphemism for he's not a rabbit but he's only just better than that. The wicket-keeper cannot be a 'nick and nudge' batsman … he must be a full blooded striker. Talent will get you so far … it's a vital and necessary platform … it must be stressed, however, it's only a base.

Number Two – Find a mentor

There are very few sportsmen who don't want their careers over again … I'm no different. If I could go back, my first objective would be to find a mentor … to link up with someone who possessed an integral knowledge of me and my craft. Wrist spinning is a particularly arduous journey. To have linked up with somebody early in my career who understood the intricacies and the psyche of my discipline would have made life as a slow bowler more bearable. Generally, young players get plenty of support and encouragement … only a few, however, will have a personal coach for a greater percentage of their time in the game. Matthew Hayden has his brother … Michael Clarke consults his boyhood coach … Shane Warne has always had Terry Jenner to bounce off. You will definitely need someone!!! Elite sport may have comprehensive internal structures in place but nothing can compare with the one-on-one relationship with a mentor who knows you and has a thorough knowledge of your discipline. I knew little about mentoring and its benefits when I played … my headstrong nature worked against me … I falsely believed I could work it out myself … there was nobody there for me when things got tough – so I internalised everything. It was a huge mistake!

Number Three – Be disciplined on and off the field

In your developing years – say from ages 13 to 20 – there will be a number of issues that have to be dealt with correctly. Peer pressure will be a factor … do not compromise your ambition just to fit in with a group mentality. If you prepare well, you give yourself every chance to play to your full abilities. If you are making development squads and being exposed to specialist coaching seminars, soak up as much information as possible and discern which most applies to your improvement as a cricketer. Enjoy the fun that can be generated from team environments and participate in the spirit of occasion but be mindful of your personal obligations. During former Australian captain Mark Taylor's formative years, coaches noted the quiet demeanour of the chunky left-handed opener from Wagga Wagga. 'He didn't say much but you sensed he was taking it all in', one former under-age coaching co-ordinator once conceded. 'Tubby' wasn't, initially, identified as a star – a hardworking stodgy opening batsman who seemed to have limitations. The same youngster went on to a glittering Test career as player and captain and was voted Australian of the Year a few years ago. His conduct during the vital embryonic stage of his career is a standout example to every hopeful. My own focus and committment as a teenager contributed to my rapid elevation from district third grade aged fifteen to first grader at sixteen. Sheffield Shield selection followed at age nineteen and an Australian cap soon after my twenty-first birthday. I was first to practise and last to leave for all of this period … some of my best net bowling performances took place in a half-light – as you'd expect, I guess?! Heh! I remember having a long talk to former Australian Rugby League player Ken McCaffery when I was eighteen and he gave me good advice:

'When you're in a dressing room getting changed for a game and you're hearing how your team-mates were out drinking or chasing girls and how tired they are ... feel good about yourself that you have given yourself every change of playing well by your preparation ... you don't have to judge them ... but you will know in your heart that you have done the right thing by yourself and your team ... go out there and reap the rewards of your discipline!'

Number Four – Have an away from the game outlet

Cricket can be addictive ... if you find that you are thinking about nothing else seven days a week, you are doing yourself a disservice and must set about establishing balance to your life. It's a cliche but 'putting all your eggs in one basket' is prejudicial to your future. I am involved in the emerging player programme at Cricket New South Wales and spend a week at the AIS Cricket Academy each August conducting the Specialist Wrist Spinners Seminar. I see the hunger first hand ... the rigid focus on 'making it'. I am part of the process that 'spits' out the Ricky Pontings, the Adam Gilchrists and the Shane Warnes. For every one of those superstars however, there are thousands who don't make it ... who are chewed up by the system ... these definitely need a fall-back situation. Even those who emerge at the other end of the development programmes, must have other things in life.

Whether it's another sporting interest … more importantly, it should be an aspect of business or society that will sustain them during or after their cricket careers. I was a chronic 'over practiser' – whether I was in form or not … it mattered little … unless I was in the nets, I wasn't happy. I had very few outside interests … I closed myself off to another career … I became anti-social. Every poor performance would intensify my resolve to practise more … I felt I must shut off outside influences … I convinced myself that the only way to succeed was to be one-dimensional. It was an irrational overview. A major reason for my erraticism in early retirement was that I had not factored post-cricket life into my playing days. Even my dedication to practise contained flaws … when I batted surrounded by netting, I played strokes … was uninhibited … free of mind … dominant. When I batted in the middle in a match situation, I was semi-paralysed by the prospect of dismissal … half-volleys held hidden perils … risks were rarely taken. Greg Chappell once remarked that I should hang netting down both sides of my cap before I went out to bat in an effort to simulate a net situation when I was in fact out in the middle. The game had consumed me … in hindsight, I should have cultivated an outlet … I should have laid a solid foundation for the cricket afterlife … when it came I was ill prepared both socially and mentally.

Number Five – Play the system!

You may be the most 'out there' young cricketer to have ever happened upon the game … you may well be 'your own man' … you may see yourself as 'non-political'. Be careful. These can be detrimental traits in your climb up the ladder. A certain personality prospers in cricket … you have to be aware of when to speak your mind and when to keep your peace. Mostly you should say very little. Gifted youngsters with a rebellious streak have a history of slower progression than those who 'do the right thing'. Anyone who has a reputation of being reliable, punctual, a hard worker and perhaps above everything, a 'low maintenance individual', will find doors open. Such a conclusion is not, obviously, confined to cricket but it particularly applies in this often understated but reasonably political game as much as anywhere. If you chose to play outside the system, be very certain that you're, at the very least, twice as good as an alternative choice. If you are not, 'play the game'!!

Number Six – Leave the game with mates!!

Team game it may well be … but cricket is very much a collection of eleven individuals who are chiefly concerned with their own contribution. To be seen as a 'team player' is to enjoy genuine respect amongst colleagues. Given the insecurity that is so synonymous with cricket, it is difficult to achieve … but not unattainable. At a New South Wales Sheffield Shield squad pre-season meeting in the early eighties, a sports psychologist was seeking to draw out of the players what they wanted most from the upcoming summer. Each member, in turn, would get up and declare that he wanted to be part of a winning Shield campaign and hopefully contribute to the cause. Six or seven had repeated this common view before opening batsman John Dyson got to his feet and delivered: 'I want to score 1000 runs this season!!!' He was immediately howled down with accusations of selfishness and not being a team player. Finally he continued: 'Say what you like but if I score 1000 runs we are going to have plenty of runs to play with and should win a fair share of games!' Dyson was right … he nakedly declared his personal goal above the team goal – he should not have been condemned for it. It is hypocritical for players to say they care little about records and statistics … and then go out and play for them. Cricket breeds self-interest … it is all about the individual in a team environment. My own career mirrored deeply rooted insecurity … too often, I played to stay in teams … good performances ensured my short-term future at test level … I felt I needed the numbers to push my case for retention. As a result of my pre-occupation with getting wickets and runs, I regret that I did not develop stronger friendships with so many players of my era. Concerned with my own play so much that I conditioned myself to live in my own world ... I worked so hard on my cricket, I had little time to create many lasting bonds with team-mates. It is my deepest regret from my time as a first-class cricketer. Friendships are what sports like cricket should be all about ... if you emerge from the game with stunning statistics and few friends, you are the poorer for it. Make close mates before you make centuries ... make sure, on retirement, you can ring up a former team-mate and invite him around for dinner. If you can't, the game has only given you so much.

Commentary Euphemisms

We've all had our disappointments in life. Before I met and married my beautiful wife, I had a crush on Miss Helena, the host of *Romper Room*. When she looked through the 'magic mirror' and said she could see Billy and Beau, Kirsty and Karen, I used to wish she'd say 'Kerry' ... just once. Then Miss Helena up and married ABC weatherman Mike Bailey. Even though we'd never met, I was devastated ... no, make that disappointed. I mean, 'Bails' might have been a great guy but – those suits! Fair dinkum, 'Bails's' threads made pallbearers look like they were dressed by Ken Done. Still, beauty is in the eye of the beholder ... whatever the dull suit. And, yeah, now of course I hope they're happy – I'm over it.

In cricket commentary it is seen as best practice to dilute what you really feel – except if you're Shane Warne, who shoots from a 708 Test-wicket hip! And even Warney adheres to the charter on occasions. Take the old chestnut 'He'll be disappointed in that shot', for example. For the last forty years it has been the go-to phrase to describe a batsman getting out to an atrocious stroke. You will hear it about fifty times this summer. Take it from me, it's not what the commentator really wants to say – but it is the middle ground that we, in the box, all look to take at certain times. Frequently the departing batsman will have been at the centre of selection speculation after a horrid run of outs and occasionally the poor fellow will have just lost all three stumps attempting a wild village yahoo swat across the line before he has opened his account. As the downcast victim trudges off, the commentator will offer: 'He'll be disappointed in that shot!' Disa-bloody-pointed? His career is now effectively over: his CA contract is lost, his marriage will deteriorate and he'll hit the bottle for the next decade … yeah, I guess he's *disappointed*!

For heaven's sake, let's stop pussyfooting around. I have determined to say at least once this summer on ABC Radio: 'That was the worst attempted stroke I've ever seen – Charlie Sheen chooses better options than that effort. He should have a good hard look at himself after that pitifully inept effort.' Yet I'll probably, in the end, settle for how 'disappointed' he is!

Another commentary euphemism to look out for is normally reserved for the defensively orientated strokeless wonder. As the aforementioned bore launches into his umpteenth full-blooded dead-batted block to silly mid-off, the commentator will opine: 'He sells his wicket dearly, this bloke!' For that please read: 'He's as boring as bat poo and I, for one, am praying that this interminable bore is fired out lbw off a thin inside edge in the next couple of minutes.' In the modern game the block-artist is a fast-diminishing species who is, nonetheless, always mysteriously given due respect by commentators despite having less entertainment value than back to back viewings of *Who Wants to be a Millionaire*?

And what about the all-encompassing description of a number eleven whose career average is fractionally below the number of women that George Michael has slept with: 'He's no mug with the bat!' I just cringe when I hear it; my face crumples like a Shar Pei when I utter it. What we should be saying is: 'This bloke is pathetic. If I was him I'd have caught a lift to the crease on the heavy roller because it will be doing its stuff within one or two deliveries anyway.'

Then there's that time-honoured lame commentary attempt to make your colleague feel his age. For example, when a statistic regarding a match played in, say, the early 1900s is being discussed, one of the commentators will say: 'That was around your time, Kerry, what did you think of so-and-so's innings?' And you in turn bleat, 'Ah, turn it up,' and to feigned laughter you both move on. It is such an absurd tack to take in the presumption of somebody actually being around so long ago ... unless you're on with Richie, of course.

Recently retired players do it toughest in the commentary box. Throughout their careers most have bristled at how easy it appears to be for those calling the game to criticise – unfairly they reckon, a great deal of the time – and how 'negatively' some of the commentators judge the Australian players. Then, having called it a day on the field, suddenly they have a microphone and a strong, almost unbendable, will not to criticise any player or do anything but speak positively of how the Australian team will extricate itself from its occasional dire situation. Any criticism of the Aussies by a former Test player is regarded in the dressing room as treason.

As recently as last summer, that great fighter, Justin Langer, was trying his hand at ABC commentary. Little 'Alfie' was asked by Jim Maxwell, 'Would you have dropped Andrew Symonds?' Five minutes later, after a character reference that would have made Mary McKillop's sainthood application look lukewarm, 'Alfie' still hadn't definitively answered the question. With experience and time, happily, they work out how it operates. Thank the Lord.

When Skull Rules the World

Sporting dreams are not the prerogative of the young … 20 odd years ago my Shangri-la was to coach the Australian cricket team.

The rough plan was to guide the Sydney University Poidevin-Gray (under 21) competition to a premiership, move on to the New South Wales Sheffield Shield squad and then the national job.

I fell at the first hurdle! It was no picnic mentoring penniless 20-year-old students, you know. Shouting beers four times in a shout of four after the match wasn't fun. Neither was fielding incoherent phone calls at one am requesting directions to that day's away venue.

And then there were your opening bowlers turning up late to a vital semi-final clash … in dinner suits! Nonetheless, I still harbour desires to plot an Australian Test triumph. Here is my game plan targeting seven South Africans who may just be a little vulnerable at the WACA on Wednesday. At least these days I'm confident Brett Lee and Stuart Clark won't be at a Bachelors and Spinsters Ball the night before.

Graeme Smith

- Has the biggest backlift of any current Test opener: 'Bing' (Brett Lee) should spear fast full inswingers looking for an lbw decision.
- Have a floating third slip for the fast bowlers: Smithy is a prolific worker through this area off an open bat face. Don't give him cheap boundaries.
- Matt Hayden to chirp: 'Haydos' and Smith have a history.
- 'Haydos' to constantly remind him that he is now in a WS Cox Plate: all that recent success in mid-week provincial class counts for nothing.

Jacques Kallis

- These days his bat pickup is slower than an ICC decision.
- 'Bing' and Mitch Johnson to release Yorkers and sandshoe crushers: they are a big chance for either bowled or lbw.
- Constantly remind him when he is on strike that his run-rate has fallen lower than the Dow Jones Index.

AB de Villiers

- Big candidate for bowled through the gate as his weight transfer can be sluggish early: 'Sarfraz' (Stu Clark) to work off cutters against him.
- Poor player of spin: bring on 'Subway' (Jason Krejza) early – even 'Pup' (Michael Clark) is worth a couple of overs when he first comes in.
- Constantly chat about what 'Warney' would have done to him: call him 'Darryl' after the much missed Darryl Cullinan.

Morné Morkel

- There will be an average of one no-ball every couple of overs: pounce on it!
- Morkel gives width to left and right handers: look to hit him square of the wicket more than down the ground.
- Right handers with good square cuts can hurt him: 'Pup', 'Punter' (Ricky Ponting) and 'Roy' (Andrew Symonds) take note!

Makhaya Ntini

- Over after over, Ntini bowls just short of the length swinging across the left handers: It's as boring as re-runs of *McHale's Navy*. Don't flash at his width: 'Haydos' to shoulder arms and wear him down.

- Right handers (particularly 'Punter' and 'Pup') must cover off stump fully as his most dangerous delivery is bowled from wide of the crease and leaves you off the deck.
- Will regularly drop onto the right-handers' pads when tired: happy birthday 'Pup', 'Punter' and 'Roy'.

Dale Steyn

- Stay side-on in defence as much as possible to him: his big wicket-taking delivery is the fast outswinger which squares you up on the half front foot looking for outside edges or bowled.
- There will be plenty of scoring options on your pads if the ball isn't swinging: be patient!
- 'Mr. Cricket' (Mike Hussey), duck his short stuff: you may have smashed that blancmange from the young girl in the LJ Hooker advertisement but your pulling on quicker pitches is suspect!

Paul Harris

- This left-arm orthodox spinner looks like Stuart Appleby but bowls like Ashley Giles.
- Attack him from the first delivery: 'Haydos' should be down the track and launching him into the next postcode.

- 'Punter' should be on, driving his drift into leg stump until he is dizzy.
- Left handers should sweat on the short offering outside off stump.
- Okay, that's the game plan, boys – now early to bed.

14 December 2008

The View from the Couch

As ABC *Grandstand* management has granted me an RTO (Rostered Test Off), I have been watching the fine television coverage from Perth on Channel Nine.

Steve Crawley and his team have put together the slickest of productions highlighted by camera techniques which allow the viewer to get up close and personal with Brett Lee's sweat droplets. The commentary squad seems to have changed less over the years than Vatican policy. Richie Benaud, at 78, is still in great form. His unique talent is ageless: the doyen is reportedly considering a new two-year contract at the conclusion of which he will take over from Bert Newton in hosting *20 to 1: Pets Who Poisoned Their Owners*.

In the meantime, the battle for the beige continues – the debonair Englishman Mark Nicholas has silky presentation skills and may have the inside running despite many in their lounge rooms thinking his name is something like Mike Nichols!

There is no South African representative on the commentary team this summer, though Tony Greig has been 'porking his corr in the corr pork' each day and doing his best to sound like 'Ox' du Randt.

The advertisements, too, have got me in. Teetotalling Bill Lawry has looked far too sober for backyard cricket – a game played best after a couple of frosties – and Ricky Ponting seemed to be endlessly extolling the energising effect of his vitamin tablets while appearing to be on Valium.

On the field, Mitchell Johnson was a star with eight first-innings wickets. Critics bang on endlessly about his release position, lack of an in-swinger and his wayward width. Meanwhile, young Mitchell continues to get a wicket every forty or so balls at an average well below the legal drinking age. Imagine if the Queenslander ever manages Alan Davidson's in-swinger and the accuracy of Wasim Akram – nineteenth-century chastity belts wouldn't keep him out! It has become increasingly obvious with Brett Lee's pace diminishing that Johnson will lead the attack to England next year for the Ashes campaign … the Poms will be intrigued – but not surprised – that the outstanding colonial quickie has a stud in his tongue. Johnson, too, revealed in a tell-all interview during the third-day lunch break that his worst habit was … biting his fingernails! Ooh ahh! Note to Fleet Street tabloids: don't bother holding the front page for potential Johnson nightclub incidents!

Apparently, too, Mitch has been strumming his guitar throughout the match with the multitalented Jason Krejza – significantly, both are in the best of form in the middle. Could somebody find Matthew Hayden a plectrum? Despite being the victim of jaffas, run-outs and umpires' eyesight that Fred Hollows couldn't improve, the champion Queensland opener looks a shadow of his former self. Hayden's game was never built on conventional technique – it was all about hand–eye co-ordination and brutality. At 37, however, those powers weaken and self-doubt can suddenly enter the room. Hayden has been the world's best opener because he unconditionally backed his ability straight out; the Australian's body language in Perth suggested he has been reduced to an each-way punter.

The selectors, depending on the result of this Test, may extend 'Matt the Bat' the option of completing the home summer – and he may yet summon a last hurrah – but the twilight is dimming.

Hayden's replacement is bound to create angst. Victoria's Chris Rogers is scoring more frequently than automatic teller machine robberies while Phil Jaques – whose back problem apparently made Quasimodo look pain-free – is not far away from playing again.

Prodigiously gifted NSW 20-year-old left-handed opener Phil Hughes, however, is destined to wear the baggy green for at least a decade or more. Do the selectors reward the 31-year-old Rogers, wait for Jaques, or bite the bullet and promote Hughes? If it was to be Rogers or Jaques, then Hughes could be withering on the vine for another three or four years … and that would be a waste of real quality. My gut feeling is that Andrew Hilditch and his co-selectors will back their instincts and introduce the 20-year-old Blue from Macksville.

Anyway, I'm off to the lounge: 'Roy' is just about to drive through that car wash without paying for the thousandth time.

21 December 2008

Frog Joke

It's amazing the longevity that can accompany certain jokes. I'm having lunch at the Sunnyside Tavern in Hamilton, Newcastle … it's an older style hotel where patrons of the front bar still wear flannelette shirts and the pub tab does regular business. My luncheon is in the dining area where I am the guest of the Hamilton Hawks Rugby Club … a strong Catholic-based organisation who play in the Newcastle-Hunter Valley competition. Michael Coughlan is the publican and the prime mover behind organising me to address members of the rugby club. I am particularly heartened by the presence of one Gary Gilmour and am struck by how well dear Gus looks. He's drinking Diet Coke and hasn't had anything alcoholic now for a few years but he's alive and his new liver appears to be functioning really well. When I last saw Gus in Newcastle it was at a fundraiser for the ailing all rounder and his life was slipping away. Since then of course he's had the organ transplant and his colouring and vitality has returned because of it. I'm sitting at my table prior to speaking and Ron Field enquires whether I'm going to tell the 'frog joke'. I say no ... it's not in my repertoire and it's a specific joke for radio cricket. I'm still mystified at the success of the only joke I've ever told on air. It was during the third one day international between Sri Lanka and Australia at the Gabba on a working afternoon in March 2006. For the benefit of those who may not have heard the joke here is a transcript:

> **O'Keeffe:** A frog goes into a bank and approaches the teller – he can tell from her name plate that her name is Patricia Whack. Miss Whack I'd like to get a $30,000 loan to take a holiday
>
> **Glen Mitchell:** Bracken to Sangakarra who leaves the ball moving away from him
>
> **O'Keeffe:** Patty looks at the frog in disbelief and asks his name. The frog says his name is Kermit Jagger; his dad is Mick Jagger and that it's okay he knows the Bank Manager. Patty explains that he will need to secure the loan with some collateral. The frog says sure I have this

and he produces a tiny porcelain elephant about an inch tall, bright pink and perfectly formed.

Glen Mitchell: Is this going to take many overs. Bracken running away from us again Sangakarra another leave

O'Keeffe: Very confused Patty explains that she'll have to consult with the bank manger and disappears into the back office. She finds the manager and says there's a frog called Kermit Jagger out there who claims to know you and wants to borrow $30,000 and wants to use this as collateral. She holds up the tiny pink elephant. I mean what in the world is this. The bank manager looks back at her and says, 'It's a nick nack Patty Whack, give the frog a loan, his old man's a rolling stone.'

Glen Mitchell: And Bracken to Sangakarra and he pushes to mid off no run.

Of course the last part of the joke is told with both Glen and I falling about during the punch line. It is an anecdote that really is dependent on a ball by ball commentator running with it and not punctuating it with anything as rude as the fall of a wicket. I was lucky this day. Some people still say to me that that joke went for overs when in fact it went for three deliveries!! Radio is all smoke and mirrors. I will probably never tell another joke on ABC Radio … basically because I haven't got another joke but it appears I will forever be remembered and am humbled by everybody's enjoyment of the 'frog joke'.

15 June 2007

Bah, Humbug!

Don't get me wrong, I'm no Grinch … but as you get older, Christmas Day gradually loses its aura. Gifts, for example, tend to reflect where you're at: judging by my meagre haul this year I am an old man who needs a change of underpants every few hours, has a body odour problem and whose facial skin is drier than Tutankhamun's.

Some things remain eternal on this day, however, like the evening television news footage showing the Australian cricketers and their families spending the day together. There, inevitably, every Christmas is Matt Hayden bowling to his lovely baby daughter in the middle of the MCG – now I'm not saying that 'Haydos' has played on too long, but there he was again this year bowling to his daughter … and her husband … and their children!

Presents and 'Haydos' aside, the highlight for me on the day is my wife's Christmas trifle. It is considered a work of art amongst the family and she guards the recipe as if it was the Coca-Cola formula. If trifle making was an Olympic event, my darling would have it all over Stephanie Rice Pudding. It has been said that she may be a little heavy-handed with the marsala content in her signature dish ... when it is presented mid-afternoon, arguments break out amongst relatives as to who is to be the designated

driver. Two helpings of the Veronica O'Keeffe trifle and you ask Andrew O'Keefe for a lift home.

On Boxing Day I am in Melbourne to work on the Test match for ABC *Grandstand*: it is the premier cricket day of our summer. On this day Victorian males trim their moustaches and put down the upcoming AFL season fixture list to watch cricket.

Though I never played in a Boxing Day Test I spent a number of Christmas Days in Melbourne during the early 1970s. We would start a Sheffield Shield match against Victoria on the 23rd of December and enjoy the 25th of December as a rest day. Cricket NSW would, year after year, book the team into the Hosies Hotel, a half-star licensed premise on Flinders Street. Now I'm not saying that Hosies was a blood house, but each year players would hold a team meeting on Christmas morning to discuss tactics on how to avoid being involved in an all-in brawl that afternoon.

The MCG is where I made my test debut in 1971 against England under the captaincy of Bill Lawry. It was the proudest moment of my sporting life, though perhaps I would have felt more part of the team if Bill had not kept calling me 'Terry' throughout the five days!

One match down in the series, Australia needed to start this year's Boxing Day match well and the skipper delivered. Ricky Pon Ting did his Chinese heritage proud with a clinical 100 on the opening day. The Pon Tings have been mining tin in the northeast of Tasmania for over a century and I'm certain they would have celebrated the achievement of one of their own with traditional oriental dignity.

Hayden's failure continues to threaten his career … the sight of one of the strongest hitters down the ground in our cricket history now reduced to a slicer to the slips cordon is sad, indeed. At his peak 'Haydos' would displace Bill Ponsford as Arthur Morris's opening partner in any best-ever Australian team. However, the big Queenslander will need to produce something special in the second dig to avoid a phone call from Andrew Hilditch. I reckon 'Haydos' has two alternatives: he can either drop his hips more positively into his attacking shots or he can try a bowl or two of my wife's trifle. Both are guaranteed to loosen limbs!

28 December 2008

Big Men Do Cry

When Graeme Smith heroically emerged from the shadows of the SCG Members' Stand last Wednesday, I didn't cry. This, in itself, was surprising because my tear ducts can generally open at the sight of a beetle floating in a pool. Men should cry more! I'm not saying I'm a cry baby but when my wife and I go to the movies to watch a chick flick, she doesn't bring tissues … she brings a towel! Compared to me, Kim Hughes was an unemotional iceberg … I would have bawled my eyes out on *getting* the Australian captaincy. I teared up when Rick McCosker went out to bat without a helmet and with a badly broken jaw in the second innings of the Centenary Test at the MCG in 1977 … and I was walking alongside him as his runner. I was sobbing so much, I almost ran him out four times in the first half hour. 'Rick the Snick' was so brave that day … his courage even touched the

Poms, whose bottom lips were trembling as they ran in to bowl. Consequently, they served him up such feeble dross and half-rat power bouncers that I made a note to myself that next time I was to bat against Bob Willis I would take strike wrapped up like a mummy.

Smith's bravery in batting with a broken left hand and a limp right elbow sat comfortably with many who came to support the legacy of the late Jane McGrath. Now that great lady was tough. How tough? Well she'd have probably even declined batting

gloves during that gripping final half hour. In another era, Jane would have faced Jeff Thomson's sandshoe crushers in stilettos! There were hundreds of tears for J. McGrath and G. Smith at the SCG this week … and everybody felt better about themselves and cricket at the end.

◈

Australia should take five fast bowlers to England for this year's Ashes defence. There are four certainties – Mitchell Johnson, Peter Siddle, Stuart Clark and Ben Hilfenhaus. The fifth could be anybody.

With a heavy heart, I can't find a place for Brett Lee from a couple of viewpoints. 'Binga' took 21 wickets at an expensive 40 runs each in 2005 and four years later is not the same bowler. Also, his best form has been after a long preparation and it is unlikely the blond paceman will have the time after his enforced layoff.

Of the other contenders, Doug Bollinger may not offer enough on the slower English pitches and Shaun Tait also misses my squad because the planets have to align for too long for him to be a consistent game breaker on softer surfaces. The final spot should go to a 'smokey'. The fastest bowler I've seen this summer is Dirk Nannes, a fiery left-arm Victorian who is both an outstanding alpine skier and fluent in Japanese. This type of chap, however, has never really bowled the Poms out over the years. Other long shots include Queensland's Ryan Harris, who is talented but diminutive, and his team-mate Chris Swan, who could swing a brick but is already 30.

The best trajectory of any fast bowler in the country belongs to an 18-year-old giant from Tamworth named Josh Hazlewood. Comparisons with Glen McGrath have already been made. At the same age, however, McGrath was batting number four for Rugby Club in the Narromine competition and bowling second change ... Did I say number FOUR? My God, now that's a long tail! This kid already has a strong pedigree, having represented Australian under 19s with distinction. Hazlewood debuted for New South Wales against the touring New Zealanders at the SCG in November last year and finished with a match analysis of 4–76 on a bland pitch. All the boxes were ticked – bounce, movement off the seam, swing, accuracy. I believe Hazlewood, even at his tender age, could handle the pressure of an Ashes tour. Australia is in transition: David Warner is an international already ... Phil Hughes is next ... and then, just maybe, the smokey, Josh Hazlewood! Come on Andrew Hilditch, back a teenager for the long haul!

11 January 2009

'Thommo' – The Fastest Bowler Ever!

I've always liked Jeff Thomson … you can't help but like him. He's raw … honest … a bloke's bloke! He's probably as close a figure to Ernest Hemingway as Australian cricket has produced … his great loves are fishing, hunting and the bar!

'Thommo' was possibly, too, the fastest bowler of all time. The shuffling run up and slinging release propelled the ball at offensive speed – he had a period between 1973 and 1976 when no batsman in the world felt comfortable against his blistering thunderbolts.

'Thommo' should have played test cricket a couple of summers before he actually did but he had an uneasy relationship with NSW cricket authorities and was continually overlooked by the selectors of the time. And this while terrorising club cricketers playing for Bankstown in the Sydney district competition.

'Thommo' was in the NSW Sheffield Shield squad at the time but found the aspects of fitness training like piggy backing fellow members up steep hills boring and unproductive. His absences from practice sessions were noted … and there was the small matter of his waywardness in the middle, as well. One of the vogue practice drills employed by SCG coaching staff at the time was to place a hoop on a good length in one of the nets and have the bowlers deliver an over of eight balls and land as many as possible inside the circle. Success rates were recorded. Not surprisingly, 'Thommo's' numbers were always poor … but, seemingly lost on coach and selectors, was the number of shattered pickets behind the nets which groundsmen had to replace the next morning. 'Thommo' was regarded as fast but 'all over the place' … funny, really, because those keeping him out of the team were much less fast and also all over the place!!

I once asked Jeff's great mate, Len 'Slippery' Pascoe, about the quickest spell he'd seen from the champion paceman. Slippery recalled: 'It was definitely playing for Bankstown against Manly Warringah at Manly Oval on a Saturday in February 1974. It was shortly before he decided to go and play for Queensland. The pitch was hard and bouncy and 'Thommo' was really letting them rip. Our wicket-keeper Ian 'Gormo' Gorman must have been forty yards back and the slips couldn't hold on to any catches they were coming so quick. Some deliveries were pitching just short of a length ... going over the wicket-keeper's head and crashing into the concrete boundary wall down the southern end on the next bounce. 'Gormo' would turn and take a couple of steps to pick up the rebounding ball. It was frightening. And some of the batsmen were coming out to bat in terry towelling hats. 'Thommo' reckoned they were only good for mopping up their blood after he'd crashed one into their heads'.

The miracle of that period was that no Sydney district player died facing this unique speedster ... oh there were a couple of fractured skulls and a number of broken arms and fingers but no deaths, thankfully.

When the English team of 1974/75 arrived to defend the Ashes, 'Thommo' was ready and so was Dennis Lillee. The Poms were swept away by this pair and so was forged the most lethal new ball combination of its era. For two years it was Lillee downwind and the fastest bowler in the history of the game running into the wind ... the captain must have been Irish!

Tragedy struck Thommo on the opening day of the first test against Pakistan in 1976 ... the big fellow had begun a scorching spell from the river end ... I was so deep in the gully, our skipper Greg Chappell was thinking of moving me in a yard or so to stop the single. Heh! 'Thommo' had Zaheer Abbas and company retreating to square leg ... I thought he'd get seven or eight wickets that day. Suddenly a half hook shot is bunted over Allan 'Fitteran' Turner's head at short leg. He turns and runs back to take the catch. 'Thommo' takes off to his right to take the caught and bowled ... there is a collision ... not blood curdling but contact nonetheless ... 'Fitteran' goes down like a bag of shit. 'Thommo' stands in agony clutching his right shoulder. I'm first on the scene from gully ... 'Forget the dead ... attend the wounded,' I shout after a brief look at 'Fitteran'. Everybody cracks up laughing except 'Fitteran', who has a headache, and 'Thommo' who has shattered his shoulder blade. Off he goes to hospital and an operation. Sadly, he is never as quick again. He recovers to resume his place in the 1977 touring team to England but, although he is our leading bowler, he never quite managed to generate the pace of the previous couple of years.

On that tour, I am his roommate ... and enjoyed his company immensely. An old 'quack' whom he trusted implicitly had advised 'Thommo' that a hot bath in Vicks VapoRub every evening would help his shoulder recover from the exertions of bowling. Diligently, virtually every night, 'Thommo' would return the room ... run the bath ... empty most of the contents of a jar of Vicks VapoRub into the steaming water ... and hop in. The stench from our room was overpowering ... neither of us caught a sniffle throughout the tour so clear were our nasal passages. Occasionally, too, after a session in the hotel bar I would forget which floor our room was on ... as the lift opened at each floor I would stick my head out the door ... if I smelt Vicks I knew I was close to home. Like a tracking device, it was.

As the years wore on, 'Thommo's' shoulder, age and slow pitches took their inevitable toll and, with 200 Test wickets and frustratingly, no Sheffield Shield, he took his long service leave. No-one who faced Jeff Thomson between 1973 and 1976 will ever forget it ... my memories should be more vivid ... except for the effect of too much Vicks VapoRub.

You Can Take the Boys out of Matraville ...

On the evidence of one delivery on a Twenty20 match this week, Jason Krejza must be the first Australia spinner chosen for the Ashes this year!

Bowling superbly for the Tasmanian Tigers against the New South Wales Blues in a must-win game, the gifted off spinner was confronted by Dominic Thornley, a ranga from Albury. Now, the talented Thornley can smack most slow bowlers around the park using a door snake. Loping in from the western end, the crew-cutted Krejza completely deceived and bowled the redhead with a jaffa! It was the ultimate dream ball for a finger spinner ...

flighted above the eyeline, dipping like a swallow and spinning from a foot or so outside off stump to take out the top of leg stump! This sort of peach is what the hard markers of off spinners demand. Without even getting close to the Muralitharan-induced cut-off point of 15-degree elbow bend, the former Fairfield boy is turning the rock more than any spinner in the country. In four years, Krejza will be at the top of his powers – an Ashes tour may even hasten that development.

◆

There's something about international cricketers who come from deep in Rabbitoh heartland: blokes like David Warner and, before him, Mike 'Roy' Whitney are the streetwise knockabouts who give the impression to outsiders that they were just one big Wednesday surf from becoming a Bra Boy! I'm glad both chose cricket. Warner and Whitney are Matraville men … upfront and immensely proud of family and background. They succeed despite encountering along the way so many of cricket's elitest tossers … like me!

I first met 'Roy' Whitney in the late 1970s at a New South Wales Sheffield Shield weekend squad trial match in Newcastle. His raw pace and aggression had attracted the attention of the selectors and the Randwick paceman was invited to strut his stuff at Newcastle University. Changing prior to the match, I asked another senior player about him and was told 'his nickname was 'Crazy' and he'd played President Cup for Souths. My God, a leaguie! Almost at once, in swaggered 'Crazy' ... in a wetsuit! 'G'day, boys, I drove up last night and slept in the car so I could catch a few waves first thing. Hello, Skull, I'm Mike Whitney,' and he shook my hand with enough force that I considered pulling out of the match with bruised fingers. Then came our day in the field. 'Crazy' bowled such pedestrian left-arm filth that I thought he would surely consider another career option at stumps. Oh no ... he walked past me laughing and joking, on the way to the showers asking where we were drinking. And there on his shoulder was a large tattoo. This was too much by half. I turned to a State team-mate and, in my most superior tone, mouthed, 'Where do they get them from?' Within two months I had been axed forever from the New South Wales team and 'Crazy' was taking the new ball with great success for the Blues and working his way towards a baggy green.

Warner looks cut from the same Whitney cloth. I met him a few years ago when he was still a schoolboy, playing on the wing for Randwick Boys High Rugby team and hooking private-school fast bowlers off his nose at off-season representative training sessions. His bravery stood out: he could take a punch but he threw plenty himself. Warner's six sixes on debut against South Africa may not quite rival recalling where you were when Kennedy was shot, but it's one sporting equivalent, at the very least.

My family gathered in the lounge room for his second tilt at the Proteas as if it were a World Cup final or the Melbourne Cup. They were not there to see someone like a Rahul 'The Wall' Dravid, who could defend O. J. Simpson with success, or a Mike Hussey, who leaves more deliveries than Federal Express. They gathered in front of the television to see David Warner from Sydney's equivalent of the Bronx. Sadly the scorecard recorded D. Warner bowled D. Steyn 7 … and, yes, maybe it was a poor option to attempt to cow shot a sandshoe-crushing 146 kph yorker from the world's fast bowler over deep mid-wicket into Moreton Bay. But that's what Matraville boys do!

18 January 2009

Boom or Bust

David Warner may boom … he may bust … and in between the little guy is going to set pulses racing whenever he takes guard. Everybody wants to be him: youngsters, gatekeepers … John Howard. One of Matraville's finest teed off on Friday again, smacking South Africa's finest test bowlers to every corner of the SCG except perhaps the Ladies' Stand Powder Room.

Of course, expectations are high – Channel Nine can't get enough of him. If Warner gets out early these days, families resume their Wii games. The jury is still out on his technique … his genuineness … his cricket smarts.

I don't know whether I'd back him to spank Ajantha Mendis on a Colombo dust bowl … or smoke a reverse-swinging Andrew Flintoff on a seaming Headingley. But, hell, on flat one-day pitches with men inside the circle, this guy is a *weapon*. When he fails, who knows whether he is playing the game people expect from him or whether there are chinks in his batting. Steve Waugh, a boom cricketer himself, once remarked early in his career that he was sick and tired of batting the way others wanted him to bat. Warner will have to arrive at that place at some stage.

Bernard Tomic, at sixteen, is a boom tennis player – most have heard of him. An unknown 19-year-old named Brydan Klein has made rapid progress under the radar to get to number 249 in the world … only his family and close friends can identify him. Klein, however, is the 'sleeper' who may just beat Tomic into the top ten. Australian cricket is littered with boom players who busted and 'sleepers' who made their way.

The 'next Bradman' tag befell Ian Craig, Norm O'Neill and Doug Walters – naturally, all came up short. Craig was too nice, O'Neill too dashing and Walters liked a drink and a smoke. All were boom youngsters. Some of our more recent champions have been 'sleepers'. Glen McGrath and Shane Warne were virtual unknowns at 18 – at that age McGrath was regularly sitting under Narromine oak trees discussing with country cricket stalwart Brian Gainsford whether to choose basketball over cricket. 'Gainy' convinced him cricket could take him around the world and make him rich, so 'Pigeon' moved to Sydney, ate takeaway and lived in a caravan.

A young Warne chose cricket above his greater love, Aussie Rules, basically because he ran like a duck and was not allowed to smoke at quarter time. Nobody linked Warne to genius when his test bowling statistics stood at a modest 1–338 after a handful of outings.

When Matthew Hayden was in the under 12s, he was built like Fuifui Moimoi yet his mother insisted her boy bat with a helmet against kids half his size … the resultant sledging toughened young Matthew.

When the Australian Cricket Academy rejected him, Hayden did not get bitter … he got better. With the doubters still outnumbering the believers, the big Queenslander found a supporter in Steve Waugh. 'Tugga' promoted his man, and the rest is history.

Plenty of boom cricketers have busted. Bob Massie took 16 wickets on debut at Lord's in 1972 and was out of Test cricket inside 12 months. Ian Davis came from the south coast town of Nowra with the 'boy wonder' tag, was treated like a boy by seniors and never fully realised his potential. Shane Lee was our own 'Ian Botham' when he emerged from Oak Flats, but injury and a certain lack of hard-nosed attitude shortened his career. Shaun Tait arrived as the 'next Thommo' with an impossible bowling action more prone to incurring physical injury than competing in the Dakar rally. Tait may boom in limited-over cricket, but sustained performance in longer forms looks a bridge too far.

Warner apart, there are other 'boomers' like the gifted Moisés Henriques, whose batting looks ideally suited to a Test team middle order yet who has recently signed a lucrative IPL contract. Neither Henriques nor Warner are 'sleepers' … whether they boom is up to them.

25 January 2009

Connaughting with Imran Khan

The picturesque Sydney University Oval No. 1 is the venue for a pre-Christmas district club cricket round. The students are locked in battle with North Sydney this day. Their overseas professional for the summer is Imran Khan, the princely champion all rounder from Pakistan. He has been engaged to play Sheffield Shield cricket for New South Wales and it seemed a perfect fit having come from Oxford University in England that he join the club that represents the most prestigious university in this fair city. Imran is a good clubman, he gets on well with his fellow players and gives 100% in every match.

In the previous district match the Pakistani experienced the sensitivity of Australians when he did battle with the University of

New South Wales. He and his Sydney University team-mates were dismissed for just 120 chasing 160 ... six of their batsmen were judged lbw including former test opener John Dyson and Imran himself. The umpire who adjudicated on all six lbw decisions happened to be the father of the Sydney University batsman who had been surprisingly relegated to second grade for this match. Dad was having none of this and took out his vengeance on his son's former team-mates. Imran was one of his victims, given out lbw to a ball which pitched outside the off stump some three feet and struck him on the thigh guard ... he took it as nobly as any prince could.

The overseas star's next match was today against North Sydney – a two-day affair and University had been bowled out for 180-odd on the first day. In reply North Sydney had reached 3–110 at lunch on this the second Saturday and were in a very strong position to take the first innings points.

During his sojourn with New South Wales, Imran was being accommodated at the Connaught, an upmarket apartment block overlooking Hyde Park in central Sydney. Rents at this high rise complex were far beyond the reach of most professionals ... Imran entertained royally on the 14th floor and did not want, from all reports, for female company.

Immie was to quote a team-mate 'as Aussie as' though he stopped short of drowning schooners of beer at the end of every match. This day at the University Oval a delicious blonde was perched high in the stand throughout the morning session ... she only had eyes for the Khan boy.

At the lunch break with Sydney University's fortune hovering on a knife edge, the radiant beauty descended from high in the stands of this grand old ground and grabbed Imran's hand as they waltzed towards the car park. His team-mates thought he may have had just ducked out for a quick sandwich in the park ... a wrong assumption ... that theory was immediately torpedoed as his late model bright red sports car accelerated out of the University car park bound for the Connaught ... you get more than lunch with Imran.

The lunch break completed, there was no sign of Imran as Sydney University took the field with only ten men ... the North Sydney total mounted slowly ... still no sign of the Pakistani. The captain at the time, Michael O'Sullivan, was less than impressed. Norths hopes of victory had risen sharply with the opposition star bowler not on the field and presumably not preparing himself professionally for a post-lunch blitz.

Thirty minutes after play had resumed the red sports car re-entered the car park and discreetly Imran slipped on to the field at deep fine leg. Within an over or so a wicket fell to make North Sydney 4–140 a tantalizingly 41 runs short of victory with 6 wickets in hand.

As the players gathered to celebrate the fall of wicket, there was an uneasiness amongst the team ... Imran approached from his boundary position, walked up to captain O'Sullivan and in his best baritone announced, 'I am ready to bowl now captain.' Without hesitation the skipper threw him the ball and said 'Alright ... I don't care what you've been up to but we've just got to win this match.'

Spearheading the North Sydney charge to victory was Graham Spring, a fine district player who had been capped by New South Wales on the odd occasion. Imran handed his cap and jumper to the umpire and there followed the most withering spell of fast bowling seen at the ground for years. Consecutive bouncers struck Spring on the shoulder before middle and off stump were picked out of the ground by a searing yorker ... four more wickets fell to Imran for just two runs in his deadly spell. His team-mates embraced him at every wicket – 5–3 in five overs and the match was Sydney University's by 20 runs.

Imran proudly led his team off the field to a rapturous ovation from fellow players and support staff. After congratulations from the Chairman and the Sydney University Chancellor, Imran was at the door of the dressing room with his kit under his arm. 'See you next week boys' was his parting remark as he bustled towards the car park. The red sports car again ignited and roared away from the University ... the blonde still in the passenger seat. The road led back to the Connaught you can be sure.

There is a strong body of support for 'connaughting' to be added to our language to describe such midday dalliances. And the Pakistani all-rounder could take full credit for its entry.

What a champion ... what a performance ... that's the way to do lunch!!

6 December 1986

Australian Cricket Handbags

The Allan Border Medal evening is like *Baywatch*. In that easy-to-follow series, whenever the lifeguards were racing along the beach, five abreast, to effect a rescue, you weren't checking out 'the Hoff'.

So it was last Tuesday night in Melbourne.

Michael Clarke could have walked semi-naked down the red carpet stuffing Pat Rafter-struck tennis balls into his jocks and no-one would have noticed. Everyone only had eyes for 'the Bingle'. What an outfit! If that Iraqi journalist had thrown one of Miss Bingle's shoes at George Bush, he'd have finally laid eyes on a weapon of mass destruction. Of course, it is a night essentially for the girls … this year, too, saw the re-introduction of the brunette

– a previously unwelcome species who went bottle for bottle with the blondes in a spectacular comeback.

I'm glad there was no AB Medal during my career, because, sadly, you are judged by your partner. I was a single man without children and, shall we say, between girl friends for a decade or so. Consequently, I could only have taken my Aunty Joan, a diminutive 70-year-old who could have drunk sherry for Australia and who put away a packet of Craven A cork tips every day of her adult life. Unlike Jessica Bratich's bikini and sarong number, a sudden wind would not have compromised Joan's neck-to-knee lace confection.

I have only attended one AB Medal ... it was a couple of years ago and proved to be a very long evening, indeed. If someone had whispered to me in the early hours that John Howard had been inducted into the Hall of Fame for his hands-on promotion of off-spin in Pakistan, I'd have wearily nodded approval.

This year's event was an anti-climax: after 360-odd days of international cricket, the best Australian player is ...er, well ... a tie!

Come on, guys ... get that sorted! The joint winners, Ricky Ponting and Michael Clarke, looked suitably underwhelmed, 'Punter' appeared to have confused Valium with his vitamin tablets and 'Pup' looked obviously tired after having carried Lara's giant necklace from the wardrobe to the vanity.

Nathan Bracken was deservedly the One Day International Player of the Year: his economical left-arm pace skills have been the banker in our limited-over team for years. 'Bracks' has carved an illustrious career out of delivering stuff people can't do anything with – a sort of junk mail postman!

Simon Katich featured in the 2009 Men of Cricket Calendar and the women inside the ballroom voted him the sexiest man in the game. His wife unofficially accepted the award on his behalf and appeared to warn the other girls to keep their fur pickin' fingers off her man's mohair. 'Kat' makes Wolverine look like a billiard ball!

The New South Wales 20-year-old Phillip Hughes won the Bradman Young Cricketer of the Year ... and two days later was announced as the Australian opening batsman for the Test tour of South Africa. Hughes has the tools to emulate the deeds of the retired great Matt Hayden – he smacks it through extra cover off the front foot, through point off the back foot and works clinically behind square leg when necessary. This left hander has one other great asset – an ability to 'find a way' in any situation.

The 36-year-old Bryce McGain maintained an understated presence at the Medal, and belatedly became a Test slow bowler by the end of the week. Selection panel chairman Andrew 'Digger' Hilditch stated that McGain was the premier leg spinner in

Australian cricket. In effect, 'Digger' reckons that in a field of one, you're the best, mate! McGain's challenge, which predecessors like Beau Casson failed, will be to prove that his stock ball is consistently genuine enough at the highest level. If the veteran Victorian is standing on AB Medal stage next February with a diamond stud in each ear and holding up the Test player of the year trophy, he will have succeeded.

8 February 2009

Musings on the Season

Our international season is over and with tough tours of South Africa and England just around the corner, it is time for some predictions and reflection:

- Victorian paceman Peter Siddle, the find of the summer, and Tasmanian swinger Ben Hilfenhaus must have supreme Ashes series with the Duke ball if the urn is to stay with Australia. Siddle has a certain John Snow element to his bowling and Hilfenhaus may just be Terry Alderman with those sharp outswingers and off cutters.
- South Australian Callum Ferguson could be the established Test number six within twelve months … with Andrew

Symonds seemingly in the dimming twilight, the Australians need an aggressive, expansive strokemaker in that important position. Ferguson's one-day performances have been exhilarating and given that he scores at about the same strike rate in four-day cricket, Ricky Ponting's Test squad will be much stronger for his promotion.

- Victorian leg spinner Bryce McGain should be drafted into the one-day international and T20 squads immediately. McGain is a proven limited-over bowler at State level: he gets people out, bowls economically and handles pressure situations. The Australians need a strike slow bowler to move forward in one-day cricket. Ponting cannot seriously think that fiddling David Hussey, Michael Clarke and Cameron White is a viable strategy. McGain could slot into the Brad Hogg role for a year or two in the short form … the Victorian also has more than a puncher's chance to get to the 2011 World Cup.

- Matthew Wade, the immensely gifted Victorian wicket-keeper, is poised to gain selection as Brad Haddin's understudy for the upcoming Ashes tour. The 21-year-old Wade has a stunning 80 catches from just 17 first-class games, plays in the Victorians' limited-over team as a pugnacious left-handed hitter … and represents the future.

With Western Australia's Luke Ronchi in a form slump and South Australia's Graham Manou not quite there with the bat, Wade should be a shoo-in for the England tour.

The Australian players can now free themselves from the pressures of their advertisements. Michael Clarke can again play tennis fully clothed with a proper racquet ... and 'Pup' will also be able to walk onto a field without a chicken leg in his pocket and not have to take KFC orders from his team-mates. And 'Punter' can rest from hitting 'Johnno' through the roof a couple of thousand times ... and 'Roy' can shower in his home rather than in a car wash. Free at last!

The biggest euphemism in cricket is the use of the word 'disappointed'. Commentators and players don't get angry these days – well not in a Setanta Ó hAilpín way – no, they get 'disappointed'.

This weekend the Australian team is 'disappointed' in drawing a one-day series with modest New Zealand. That's the sailing equivalent of sharing Sydney to Hobart line honours with a tinnie. And they're only 'disappointed'!

Disappointment is not confined only to the dressing room, either.

An international batsman, with his whole career on the line after a succession of failures, will lose middle and off stump to an undisciplined slog across the line. As the unfortunate trudges off, possibly into oblivion, a commentator will blurt: 'He'll be disappointed in that shot'. Thank you, Captain Obvious!

Cricketers, past and present, rarely get too animated – it's not the nature of the individual or the game. I'm no different. When my wife presented me with our first child a couple of decades ago, the best I could manage to her in the delivery room was, 'Err … well done!' What a cretin! In my defence, it's the cricketer in me. You always restrain yourself … it's an unwritten law. Be measured at all times. Always stay underwhelmed.

Should a team-mate get a double century on debut at Lord's, you walk up to him, tap him on the shoulder and murmur … 'batted!' Had Howard Florey, on discovering penicillin, entered a room of cricketers he'd have been greeted with a nod of approval and a solitary understated … 'discovered!'

Brad Haddin was 'disappointed' that Daniel Vettori raised the controversial Neil Broom dismissal at a press conference. And recently Simon Katich was 'disappointed' that Michael Clarke was disappointed that the team song – which takes 19

seconds to belch out – had not been sung after five hours of celebration.

I'm sure that there would have been ten Australian cricketers who were 'disappointed' in Greg Chappell when he ordered the under-arm against the Kiwis all those years ago. No-one was gutted, ropeable, or thinking of putting one on misguided Greg's chin. They were simply 'disappointed'. If Australia should lose the Ashes this winter to the dear old Poms, I want Ricky Ponting to not say that the performance was 'disappointing'. Awful ... lamentable ... pathetic ... anything but the 'd' word!

15 February 2009

A Marvellous Innings

When the great Don Bradman was dismissed, newspaper banners simply read 'He's Out!' This week it became public that Richie Benaud was retiring from cricket broadcasting next year … 'He's Going!'.

That's how big a story it was and will become. No more Richie: it's unthinkable … and some have only just got over Brian Henderson calling it a day. Institutions do that to people.

Let's be frank, however: Richie has had a better run than *The Mousetrap*! Perhaps it was time. The veteran 'Westie made good' has informed, entertained and amused us for more than three decades. Richie deflects the gushing acclaim with private admissions that he has been plain lucky – as a player and as a commentator. Everyone agrees, nonetheless, that the man has made his own luck … and he is irreplaceable!

The polished and contrastingly verbose Mark Nicholas will undoubtedly get first shot at the 'off-white'. And Mark would like to let people know that he is not Mike Myers! 'Yeah baby', whatever you say, Austin.

It is acknowledged that everybody knows Richie but only a select few really know him. Thousands of Sydneysiders over the years have screamed 'Onya Richie' as Coogee's most famous resident – Jeff Sayle apart – has cruised the streets in his Sunbeam. Ninety-nine per cent of the country would not know his wife's name. Colleague Ian Chappell regards Richie as being as close as a father – it is said 'Chappelli' chooses not to swear in front of him out of respect. Richie has been the commentary team captain forever – Channel Nine should formally retire the role in recognition of his tenure.

Over the years there have been some memorable Benaud quotes – one particular favourite during a break in innings was: 'Frankly, I would have thought that using the light roller on that pitch would have the same effect as a koala doing a *pas de deux*'. Or the commentary with Michael Slater, which went something like :

Slater: 'The bowler thought he was through him but the batsman has got an inside edge on it and it has just snuck past leg stump.'

Benaud: 'Michael, there are a few words ending in "uck" in the English language but I am pretty sure the bowler wasn't thinking of one starting with "sn"!'

And he has been a man to hold his mouth at the right time. Richie's pregnant pauses often have longer gestation periods than elephants ... the fellow is more measured than long jump pits.

My own experiences with the great man have been significant. In the 1990s I was an occasional commentator for the network on domestic limited-over matches ... in fact, I was perhaps the oldest up-and-comer in cricket broadcasting history. Richie and I worked together on a dozen occasions. One slow Sunday during an interstate match at the Gabba, the doyen and I were together at the coffee urn. Richie asked if he could have a word. After a lifetime of admiring his style and expertise, I was overcome that this icon wished to share a gem. 'I notice ...' he began slowly, 'that you have a tendency to laugh at your own jokes?' 'Oh yes ... it's my trademark, Rich!' I gushed. The famous Benaud bottom lip curled and broke like a Bondi dumper as he winced: 'Oh ... really?' before gliding off looking more than a little perplexed. It was from that moment on that I realised that my commentary future may be in radio.

In life you are often linked to a number. Bradman was 99.94; Michael Jordan was 23; Johnny Farnham was one ... is the loneliest number that you'll ever know. Sorry, I can't help myself. Richie Benaud's number legacy will forever be two for 222! Every time that score line presents itself, people will attempt their 'Benaud': 'It's tchoo for tchoo tchoo tchoo.' And everybody will fall about in good-natured laughter.

The Sydney Cricket Ground Trust successfully conducted Jane McGrath Pink Day during the Sydney Test in January. As a farewell gesture to the papal presenter, the SCG should have the Richie Benaud Shirt Day when every male has to wear a white cricket shirt with the collar up and the first four buttons undone – his playing days trademark. The ladies should be encouraged to wear beige or cream on that day. I reckon it's a winner.

No one has attempted or should ever attempt to imitate his commentary style … it should be nationally heritage listed. I've already started shredding buttons for the potential Benaud Shirt Day … see you there!

22 February 2009

St George Team of the Century

St George Cricket Club turns 100 this summer and has announced its Team of the Century.

Sir Donald Bradman – who, surprisingly, registered for seven summers with Saints – captains a crack squad that includes Arthur Morris, Bill O'Reilly, Ray Lindwall, Norman O'Neill, Brian Booth and me! I'm suitably embarrassed to be mentioned in the same breath as some of my team-mates but it would initially be a pleasure to turn up at Hurstville Oval to walk onto a cricket field shoulder to shoulder with such superstars.

And how much fun would you have over the weekend? I mean, after the match on the Saturday night you could go schooner for schooner with O'Reilly and Lindwall up at Shanney's Hotel.

Then Morris would take you for a meal and some of his finest red wines. Later you'd hit the nightclub scene with O'Neill and seek salvation for your sins in the front row of a church listening to a Booth sermon on Sunday morning. Club cricket's complete 48 hours!

On the downside, you wouldn't contribute much on the field. Weeks would pass and you'd never get a bat. The Don would string double century after double century … and then Lindwall and O'Reilly would take all 10 wickets between them every innings.

You'd spend the whole season never batting once and never bowling an over. The only time anybody would know you were in that team would be your inset in the team premiership photo. You'd be the inset because after a while you'd stop turning up on time for matches and photo shoots. You'd drift into the ground late on match day with a slab of beer and sit on the hill, occasionally shouting, 'Shot, Don!' or 'Bowled, Tiger.' The club would suspend you for indiscipline and you'd finish the summer captaining the seconds.

Your admiration for the Don would turn to resentment. You'd initially want to play as much sport against the legend as you could: each week, at his invitation, he'd flog you at squash, tennis, golf and snooker. Then, when you sought solace at a licensed premises, there he'd be, drinking lemon squash and wooing everybody in the bar with his skill on the piano. For no rational reason you'd end up hating him.

At cricket practice every Tuesday and Thursday afternoon, the Don would eventually decide to see how he'd go in the nets facing you with a door snake instead of a bat ... and smugly whip your best leg spinner regularly through mid-wicket with that sausage of sand.

You'd try to sledge him about not averaging a century in Test cricket; tease him about not picking a wrong 'un from an English leg spinner in his last Test. 'That's like failing to detect body odour in a taxi driver,' you'd venture.

The Don would laugh off your taunts and take you out for an afternoon on the ... tea! He'd give you stockmarket tips – which you'd ignore, only to see them soar to 500 per cent of their original value – and would offer to install a water tank at your home so you could improve your batting hitting a golf ball with a stump against it.

You'd invite him to your wedding and women's magazines would pay him big bucks for the photos of him leaving the church. You'd go with him to shopping centres for autograph signing sessions – he'd be mobbed and you'd end up discussing your feelings with a McDonald's casual on smoko break. Still you're playing club cricket with the Don: how good is that? ... I guess.

Doriemus Delivers New Carpet

It was the first Tuesday in November, 1995 ... Melbourne Cup day ... I was alone in my lounge room, watching the lead-up events on television. My good wife was at work ... my sons at school. Occasionally I would gaze depressingly at the carpet ... yes, the carpet. Halfway through the year, I had decided that the light brown just had to go. Discoloured ... stained ... worn ... and emitting a stale smell which pervaded the home. There was also the hallway and three bedrooms to be recovered. A carpet jar was initiated ... odd notes or any unexpected windfalls were to be stuffed and sealed into that container. We had received a quote of $3,200.00 ... it seemed fair and reasonable. Months passed ... money was tight ... the jar gathered dust and not much else. December was targetted for the quote to be accepted. Significantly, I had opened the jar that morning … all up there was just $400.00 … enough for linoleum, perhaps … and one square metre of shag pile, at best. Could I risk the jar on the Melbourne Cup? No … Veronica would be devastated … she is such a rational … considered person. Gambling everything on a nag is not her way. She's not here though … she can't argue her inevitable sensible reasons for not punting. I'm watching the lead-up races … the track is favouring horses with form in rain affected going. Suddenly, I'm focussing all my attention on the Cup … I've always had my share of luck in the famous two miler. Why not again, today. I have a bank – the carpet jar!!! My rationale is simple – I have to back the winner straight out and it has to pay better than 8/1 … that will give us fresh carpet!! After three hours of deliberate study of the form, I have narrowed it down to three … Quick Ransom, Vintage Crop and Doriemus.

Every year I am drawn to the overseas imports who come to pinch our Cup. Quick Ransom looks a real two miler and has Mick Dittman aboard – if I was a horse and Mick was riding me, I'd 'put in' for the whole race … he uses the persuader with the same subtlety as Lance Klusener uses his bat. Dermott Weld, a canny Irishman who could train footballers to be celibate, will have Vintage Crop ready to run a big race – old 'Dermie' spins the 'blarney' during the week before the race and I hang off every syllable ... must be my Irish blood. And then there is Doriemus ... Lee Freedman trained ...piloted by 'Australia's Lester Piggott' Damien Oliver and an absolute 'nob' in the wet. Fifteen minutes before post time, I grab the jar ... jump into the car ... drive coldly but calculatingly to the South Hurstville TAB ... open the jar ... and without a hint of self doubt, place $400.00 on the nose of ... Doriemus. Five minutes before the start of the race, the wife arrives home having picked up my sons seven-year-old Daniel and five-year-old Thomas. I declare what I have done. The mood of the room changes ... laughter ceases ... the boys cannot help but notice Mum's demeanour has darkened. They're off! I'm cool ... Doriemus is back in centre field ... a number of horses in front of him ... but 'he's travelling'. At the 600 metre pole, Oliver begins to stoke the five-year-old gelding up ... Doriemus passes a couple of weakening horses ... he's wide ... very wide ... the going on the inside might be a little worse. Good move, 'Olly'. In the straight, he's out in the middle of the track and mowing them down ... he's got the lead ... 250 metres to go! I'm out of the chair ... I'm riding him as hard as I can ... I'm shouting at the television ... the boys are frightened ... Dad's out of it ... suddenly my wife's out of her chair ... we're riding together, Go Doriemus ... GO... GO ... 50 metres to go ... he's out by four lengths … GO… GO … nothing's coming. He's Home! Yes!!! My wife and I embrace … the boys join in for a family cuddle … the dividends flash up … $10.20 a win … multiplied by 400 … that's a net to me of $3,680.00.

The carpet salesman arrives the next day. The carpet is laid the following week. I'm the King of the House … and to think, there had been doubters?!? Thank you, Doriemus!

Duking It Out

Whoever swings the Duke cricket ball the most will win the 2009 Ashes. In full flight, the Duke is a curious piece of leather … like Rock Hudson, it can look straight but isn't. No cricket ball in the world reverse swings like the Duke!

In the 2005 series the English fast bowlers triumphed with a lethal combination of conventional and reverse swing … all the while chewing on a lolly known as the Murray Mint. Now while I'm not saying that the condition of the ball was altered by the prolonged application of 'spit and polish' by the Poms, I have not seen such movement before or since. In my day, if there had been a sweet that could make the ball spin I'd have had rotting teeth and weighed 200 kilos but, if a mint worked, I'd have sucked them 24/7.

For Australia to retain the urn, a number of crucial battles – many of them centred around the Duke – have to be won. Let's look at the key skirmishes.

Brett Lee v. The England top order

Lee's first innings spell against the English Lions in the warm-up game at Worcester confirmed his fitness and danger. The combination of an abrasive pitch plus some concerted 'work' on one side of the Duke ball and the scene was set ... enter 'Binga'! His reverse-swinging sandshoe crushers at 150kph proved as difficult to handle as a Bob Dylan interview. The Poms will be concerned that the Cardiff pitch is regarded as dry and abrasive and once 'Binga' sees the ball 'tailing' back into the right handers after 40 or so overs, he grows another leg! Alastair Cook, Andrew Strauss and Ravi Bopara are a class top three – all are outstanding players off their pads. Lee averaged over 40 runs per wicket in his two previous Test campaigns in England ... basically because his inability to maintain a consistent line has been punished. Bopara is as good a leg side player as Greg Chappell or Mark Waugh – should Lee drift anywhere near middle and leg stump against the England number three, the Aussies will be chasing more leather than Pinky Tuscadero.

Phillip Hughes v. The English fast bowlers

Steve Harmison booked a spot for the Cardiff Test by snaring Hughes twice with bouncers in the Worcester match. The English plan to beat the 20-year-old prodigy is simple: no width, plenty of chin music and eternal inswingers. Hughes' technique of staying inside the ball and following bouncers with his hands is so forged that it will be almost impossible for him to alter it over the next six weeks. James Anderson, Andrew Flintoff, Stuart Broad and Harmison will all be shaping the ball back into the left hander and giving him at least two or three short deliveries per over – Hughes is a cutter not a hooker. If the bouncers are pinpoint accurate, Hughes is in trouble. Should the Poms get the line wrong and Hughes can free his arms to execute his trademark cut shot, the Australian team and the Macksville Hotel will be more than happy.

Mitchell Johnson v. Kevin Pietersen

Johnson failed to swing the Duke in the first innings at Worcester … perhaps he should research how Wallis Simpson did it all those years ago. So much is expected of the athletic Queenslander that were he to struggle with the new ball, it would be a real body blow to Ricky Ponting's campaign. To be brutal, Johnson has a low slinging action and a limper wrist than Mr Humphries. He is often wayward and only occasionally genuinely swings the ball

... nonetheless he has a huge heart, bowling nous and extreme pace. Plus he gets wickets from nowhere. The lithe southpaw is dominant on pitches that have carry through to the wicket-keeper ... if the Poms prepare low, slow 'nothings', Kevin Pietersen – at his best the most dangerous batsman in the world – is there waiting to pump the Aussie all over the park.

The Ricky Ponting and Michael Clarke leadership

You could argue Ponting and Clarke are the two best batsmen in the team ... and perhaps the worst players of swing. Again, how England move the Duke is a big factor. Ponting often gets his weight transfer wrong and goes 'hard-handed' at the outswinger while Clarke's had problems with the moving ball in England on past visits. The captain and vice-captain have to score heavily this series at number three and five. And they have to be a mature and tactically aware captain and vice-captain. Ponting must accept a hostile media, biased crowds and England's regular use of substitute fielders. Should 'Punter' be run out by a swooping, recently naturalised Usain Bolt, the captain has to shrug his shoulders, offer a 'nice pick up, Bolty' and graciously move off. While Ponting is conservative and occasionally looks perplexed when things are going wrong, Clarke is aggressive and intuitive. How this pair blends is a significant Ashes moment.

Brad Haddin and those outside edges

Haddin's success with the bat at number seven and with the gloves is a vital factor in the Australia game plans. 'Hadds' may not be 'Gilly', but, on the better batting surfaces, he can hurt opponents just as much. However, the moving ball has always been a problem for the New South Welshman. And, on the evidence of

Worcester, England intend to rough him up with bouncers every time he comes to the crease. If the Poms can get the Duke to 'talk', Haddin will be under enormous pressure. His 'keeping, too, has attracted scrutiny. Two glaring dropped catches to his right hand in the England Lions match would not have gone un-noticed by team management. English conditions test the wicket-keeper as much as those of the subcontinent. If Andrew Hilditch and his co-selectors were completely satisfied that Haddin was the long-term answer behind the stumps, they would have chosen a batting/keeper like Matthew Wade or Tim Paine as the reserve stumper on this tour. Instead, the panel selected Graham Manou, the best gloveman in the country. It was a message.

5 July 2009

Skull's Ashes Tour Diary: From the Road

Tuesday

My Ashes adventure is about to start. I will be hosting 90 Australians on a 17-day tour to support Ricky Ponting's squad against the might of England. I have not been to the 'Old Dart' for 30 years. The trip does not begin well. Somehow I have managed to miss my plane by a whole day and will take a virus into a 23-hour flight to London. By Singapore I look and feel worse than the corpses in *Thriller*. Pet pigs in the hold have requested masks. I am sitting next to Les, who runs a TAB in suburban Melbourne … he tells me there's no money in TABs; then again he's about to spend three weeks in Europe. I've taken copious amounts of legal drugs yet I can't sleep. My fear of flying has reached the stage where I intend to seek counselling – any slight turbulence and I reach for the mobile phone just in case I have to speed-dial the wife for a final goodbye. If the Captain broadcasts a fasten seat belt warning I ask the stewardess where the black box is so I can sit next to it … they always find the black box!

Wednesday

My airship arrives at London's Heathrow at 5.30 on the morning of the first Test. I have to be assisted off the plane because my balance is so badly affected. It is déjà vu. The last time I landed in London was in 1977 as a member of the Australian Ashes team … I was not quite myself that day, either, having finished a creditable third behind Doug Walters (43 cans) and Rod Marsh (42 cans) in that infamous drinking competition. Times change, thankfully.

Suddenly I am in a limousine and being whisked to Cardiff to brief my touring party about the first day. My Welsh driver, Eiffion, is so proud that his country is hosting a cricket test but I sense he doesn't really care if England lose. You see, the Welsh and the English do not like each other … in the same way as the Irish and the English do not get on … or the Scots and the Poms

… or the English and the French. Fair dinkum, if feuding was a World Cup event, the English trophy cabinet would be bursting.

We're seated at the Swalec Stadium and greeted by the news that England will play two spinners and Ben Hilfenhaus has been preferred to Stuart Clark. 'Punter' Ponting and Clark are mates – they play golf together – yet I sense that despite Clark's great test record, Punter doesn't see a strike bowler in him. The England batsmen are hitting regular boundaries. Ravi Bopara is not enjoying a concerted attack on his Adam's apple by the Aussie quick men and then in comes Kevin Pietersen, a man whose head looks too big for his body. The pitch is a belter … only Hilfenhaus is getting the ball to move through the air. Nathan Hauritz is, as expected, already being compared unfavourably by the commentators with Shane Warne … big-hearted Peter Siddle gets two late wickets and honours are declared even after day one. The crowd behaviour has been exemplary – the Poms watch cricket well. So well, in fact, that they are rated number one in the world at the caper. I do not believe anyone was ejected from the ground and even maiden overs were generously applauded in the last hour of play.

Thursday

My health has worsened but I'm at my post for the start of play. I'm having coffee with Steve Siddle – a woodchopper from

Morwell and the proud father of Peter – who tells me his son is not comfortable with the feel of the Duke in his hand. This is not good news, as that quirky six-stitcher will inevitably decide the series. Next I'm chatting to Keith Warne who tells me his son Shane is playing cards in Las Vegas. Damn – even the sighting of 'Warney' at an English cricket ground would make their batsmen nervous.

The England tails wags annoyingly and to the surprise of many Hauritz is turning and bouncing the ball. I reckon 'Hauri' could, against all the odds, be an unlikely hero by the end of the game. We're chasing 435 and Phillip Hughes is dismissing some juicy pies from Stuart Broad through point with his trademark cut shot. Then on comes Freddie Flintoff to spoil the party. Suddenly the Hughes doubters tell me that the 20-year-old has technical and mental problems with the short ball. So did Walters but he still managed to pulverise attacks for over a decade at international level.

Soon I'm chatting with Brendan 'Bushy' McCardle – perhaps the biggest cricket tragic Australia has produced. We agree that because we are so ordinary at Twenty20 cricket that Greg Shipperd, the winningest Twenty20 coach in the country, should be given the reins for our next campaign and Ponting, Michael Clarke and Michael Hussey should be discarded. After only drinking coffee! In the middle Ponting and Simon Katich are batting like Don Bradman and Arthur Morris. Ponting's footwork would have made Michael Jackson look like a club foot and Katich's hands have the deftness of David Copperfield.

Friday

Australia march to a first-innings advantage before rain stops play after Ponting and Katich centuries. Clarke smashes 80 in a long partnership with the respected Marcus North. Around the ground the twentieth rendition of 'Jerusalem' is completed – just 80 to go. I meet Greg Hughes, the father of Phillip, and his pride is bursting. His boy plays Test cricket for Australia and this banana farmer is enjoying every second of it. Greg tells me that his wife is Italian and that Phillip played his stint with Middlesex on an Italian passport. I'm heading back in the bus to our hotel … my condition is improving. I can't wait to see Nathan Hauritz bowl Australia to victory on Sunday.

Sunday

My health has improved – I am now only critical – still, I'm the tour leader and a condition of that role is go hard or go home! In England you only drink pints … one of our party was seen coming back from the bar carrying half pints and was roundly booed.

We take 19 wickets in this first Test; the Poms take a meagre six and a draw is declared. Fair dinkum, the gerrymander is alive and well. In a gripping final day Ben Hilfenhaus swung like Tarzan, Mitch Johnson bowled like Jane and with the match on the line 'Punter' went North and our chances went south. Nonetheless, the Welsh had pulled off a great Test hosting.

Mel Slesser, a lovable window repairer from Brisbane, had the best story from day five. Now Mel could have been an extra in *The Adventures of Barry McKenzie*: his choice of attire every day is a green and gold T-shirt, green stubbies, green thongs and a green and gold floppy hat with corks dangling from its sides. Mel recounted that after ordering a few drinks that day from the bar the barman had asked, 'Where are you from, then?' Con men could do pretty well in Wales. Then there were our two most enthusiastic Collingwood AFL supporters who, during play, launched into a rousing rendition of 'Good Old Collingwood Forever' dressed in Magpie shirts when Paul Collingwood turned and got his cap at the end. Poor deluded fool!

Tuesday

I am up just after sunrise to try and walk off my lurgy and bump into our W. G. Grace lookalike, Bernie Moynahan from Victoria, who is on a gut-wrenching road run. Bernie – who had a brain tumour removed last year – tells me later that day over several pints of bitter that he captains Hoppers Crossing 7th grade and has done so for 25 years. Bernie is training because he does not want to be too unfit when pre-season workouts for his club begin … next week! Now that is what cricket is all about.

Our bus travels to London with sightseeing stops in Bath and Stonehenge. The latter is an overrated collection of rocks in the middle of nowhere where giants used to play cricket 5000 years ago. Visitors are given mobile phone-like contraptions that you punch to get information about the boulders. Apparently, during his 2005 visit, Shane Warne attempted 40 texts on his!

Thursday

We arrive at Lord's, or 'HQ' as the Brits like to call it. Yesterday I enjoyed our official tour of the ground where our guide, a four-foot Irish leprechaun named Michael, had pointed out Paul McCartney's house adjoining the Old Father Time stand side. He also related that the former Beatle complains to the MCC if balls are hit into his backyard. Paul did not enjoy the Twenty20 World Cup when Chris Gayle and Ross Taylor both deposited six-stitchers into his Octopus's Garden.

Out on the ground Andrew Strauss wins the toss and England bats on a belter. The first two sessions are agony. Strauss may look like a council water meter reader but he has the touch of a midwife. We are lamentable. Johnson is bowling a serious assortment of filth, Brad Haddin is keeping like Edward Scissorhands and Nathan Hauritz dislocates his spinning finger – which is a little like saying Douglas Bader has torn a calf muscle! By stumps we have fought back through the heart of Hilfenhaus but the Poms have the advantage.

Dave Flanders, a gentle giant from Broadmeadows, Victoria, is a man whose Geelong Cats sleeveless footy jumper is sewn to his body. Big Dave has had his photo taken with the gorgeous Lara Bingle and has already shown it to 600 people including five visually impaired. Dave has tickets to the *Jersey Boys* live show in the West End and the Prince Edward Theatre is jumping that evening. No one there is under 50 … inhibitions are out the window … and so was rationality. Frankie Valli is encouraging us males to 'Walk like a man, talk like a man' … while singing like a sheila.

Friday

The English tail wags to a very respectable 425. Ponting's animated gum-chewing technique has reached Olympic class. So much so, that zoo-keepers are showing baby giraffes a video of Punter's chomping to encourage correct jaw movement. The two teams and their entourages meet the Queen in front of the Long Room at lunch-time ... the English support staff is so large that play resumes a half hour late. Clouds hang heavily over Lord's and it's payback time! All those sins by Dennis Lillee and Jeff Thomson are righted! Strauss has ordered a bouncer barrage and Freddie Flintoff, Stuart Broad and company are attacking our throats – and we don't like it. Very few Australian batsmen use the crease well when hooking and this deficiency is clinically exposed ... five men perish to the hook! By stumps we are in danger of losing the match ... it's time for a drink. Send her down, Huey!!

July 2009

Accentuate the Positive!

General Custer could have done with Australian cricket coach Tim Nielsen towards the end of the Battle of Little Big Horn: 'Look, you're going to be annihilated, mate, but at least you know now what you should have worked harder on,' the ever-positive Tim would have offered.

In his recent press conference utterances, never-angry Tim seemed to have the view that trailing 0–1 in the Ashes series is a positive! What the …?

Fair dinkum, couldn't Nielsen just say with some emotion after a loss that the team played like muppets, that the replacement options are thinner than Calista Flockhart and that, unless we pull our fingers out, we're going to lose that damn urn?

English team insiders believe they'll win the series 3–0. I'm not a 'sack the lot' kind of a guy, but after Lord's I believe changes are a must. Performances in the current outing against Northamptonshire shouldn't count for too much. Form against county teams can be misleading. You don't win a race at Bong Bong and truly believe you're a Cox Plate contender. It is time to panic! With that in mind, selector on duty 'Skull' would choose this eleven for Edgbaston (in batting order):

S. Katich, S. Watson, R. Ponting, M. Clarke, M. Hussey,

B. Haddin, G. Manou, N. Hauritz, P. Siddle, S. Clark,

B. Hilfenhaus

In: S. Watson, G. Manou, S. Clark

Out: P. Hughes, M. North, M. Johnson

It was tough to leave out Phil Hughes but the English pace men have his measure at the moment and this outstanding youngster may not have the time in the next few weeks to sort out an effective counter to the concerted bodyline attack. Having watched an informative Channel 7 story on Hughes a couple of months ago, I blame his mother's flowerbed for his footwork shortcomings. You see, when young Phil was flaying his father, Greg, and his brothers in backyard games, the bigger fixed scoring zones were on the off side. Hence his penchant for the cut shot. The side fence through point was an easy four … while striking the clothesline pole at mid-on was worth 25 … and 50 on the full! Phil apparently scored the odd two-ball century. Sadly, Mum's rose garden was just behind short square leg and only scored two runs if you turned a ball into it. Hughes dealt almost exclusively with the off side fence … and the Hills Hoist!

Golden boy Shane Watson would be my opener with Simon Katich. Yes, I know, Watto had a cushy ride, but if you strip away the facial moisturiser, the hair gel and the eternal tan, Watto's straightness could make Fred Nile blush. The Aussies need technical purity at the top of the order. Plus, the Queenslander is, by the lunar calendar, just ten days away from straining a groin plucking nasal hair – now is the time to pick him.

Mitchell Johnson is down: slow English pitches punish lack of precision with the ball and Mitch has leaked too many boundaries with his waywardness. He is still capable of miracle balls but the frequent 'pies' rob Ponting of the chance to build pressure. Johnson has found that a leg stump line in the Old Dart is more expensive than airport parking.

And his mother's untimely 'never forget, I still love you, mate' statement has reportedly upset his psyche. From all reports the admirable Justin Langer often used the same line whenever his great mate Matthew Hayden was dismissed and 'Haydos' never seemed unduly upset. Most pundits are banging on about the lowness of Mitch's slinging left arm ... I have watched countless tapes of his Lord's bowling spells and reckon that it is the lowness of his right arm and shoulder that is causing all the problems. Johnson needs to hold the right side of his body more upright at release. Hopefully, Troy Cooley is on the case.

Nonetheless, the strangely under-rated Stuart 'Sarfraz' Clark deserves his chance ... 'Sarfraz' wobbles the ball, bowls stump to stump and has the trajectory that will compromise 'nickers' like Ian Bell, Paul Collingwood and Ravi Bopara.

Brad Haddin should be the number six and not have to worry about the wicket-keeping duties ... his brilliant batting at Lord's somewhat glossed over the nutmegs and curious tardiness to his left-hand side when 'keeping. South Australian gloveman Graham Manou, with hands as steady as Fred Hollows, would lift the outcricket and set the required catching standard for what seems a somewhat nervous slip cordon. Sadly, Marcus North makes way for Manou despite a stellar record in his short test career – doubts nonetheless remain about his ability to play quality spin at number six.

Okay, my team is unlikely to get the nod for Edgbaston, but if we go two–nil down in the series, with two to play, you can bet coach Tim will be saying it is 'a perfect position to draw the best out of the boys'.

26 July 2009

Carport Cricket

After nearly a decade of contests this was to be the decider. There could only be one champion team in O'Keeffe Carport Cricket … I was ready … so were the other three. The pitch had not changed much through the ten years of competition … concrete rarely does!!

We don't have a garage … we have a carport. It's roomy and accommodates two vehicles – in single file. We have lawn behind our house but there is a clothes line in the middle so backyard cricket was out of the question … the guy who designed clothes lines must have hated cricket, you know – Hills Hoists have been one reason young Australians have occasionally taken to hanging round shopping malls instead of whiling away hours in brotherly cricket confrontations!

Over the years, cricket at the O'Keeffes' has been all about the carport and some mighty battles it has hosted. Between the ages of 10 to 16, my sons Daniel and Thomas were keen 'carport Pontings'. We played Test matches – to make even sides of two, Jonathon 'Jono' Gardner joined us. 'Jono' is the same age as Daniel and they are great mates. They were one team ... Tom, a year or so younger than both, was my partner. Our tests were hard-fought affairs ... with plenty of pressure.

The rules were simple. Each test was a traditional four innings affair. The concrete pitch was just 12 yards long. Just short of a good length lay a two feet by two feet grease patch ... while the concrete surface was true and consistent, the same cannot be said about the grease patch. We played with a tennis ball ... the less hair on it the better. There was no running between the wickets. Batsmen were either opening or at first drop ... with two a side, you have no middle order or tail – that's good for the self-esteem, at the very least. Every time you hit the ball, you scored one run ... hit the ball past a rough line (seven yards in front of the stumps) and you had two ... strike it along the ground past the stumps line at the bowler's end for a boundary. Take a risk and strike it over that line on the full and you had six. The concrete wall at the back of the batting end of the carport was an automatic wicket-keeper. Snick it onto that slab of bricks on the full and you were out. Two garbage bins could be used as extra fielders – they were inevitably placed close on the off and onside respectively.

You could bat forever. Lbw was a manner of dismissal but the batsman had to agree he was plumb or he got the benefit of the doubt. Strangely, there were very few disputes. For six years, we must have had close to a hundred Test series ... it was the happiest and most uncomplicated cricket I have ever played, anywhere!!

Please find a form guide on the combatants:

Daniel O'Keeffe

Genuine all rounder ... capable of sharing the new tennis ball and batting in top two?! Very good outswing bowling action. Not a big spinner of the ball – it's a genetic thing, I'm told. Fine off-side striker. Not strong off his legs. Clever reader of wrist spin – spots variations very quickly. Sound temperament. Excellent team man. Good judge of lbw – when he's bowling! Sure catcher – particularly off his own bowling.

'Jono' Gardner

Promising soccer player ... comes from a soccer playing family. Wicket-keeper in under age cricket. Delivers medium pace 'nothing' balls ... tries the odd leg cutter. Always attempts to hit grease patch when bowling. Useful batsman ... tall and gets well forward. Can't pick my wrong-un or flipper. I love bowling to Jono. Sorry, I digress. Very competitive ... shares a strong team ethic with Daniel. Can get nervous when batting close to a win. Reacts well to sledging. A thorough gentleman. Great bloke.

Tom O'Keeffe

His favourite sports are swimming and surfing. Cricket appears too slow for him. Stiff upright stance. Likes to hit the ball powerfully. Plays his shots from the outset. Hits across the line. In other words, a compulsive slogger. Handy pace bowler with slinging 'Jeff Thomson' like action … possesses the 'sand shoe crusher'. Sadly, has a very obvious slower ball – he keeps trying it, nonetheless, and I keep wearing the batsmen's inevitable bludgeoning swipe directly in the groin at shortish mid-on. Very single-minded. Resilient under pressure … has nerves of steel. An impact cricketer – when he's involved with bat or ball something seems to happen. Tom once admitted to me that he rarely blocked the ball because he didn't want to look a 'nerd'?!?!

Kerry O'Keeffe

Well past his best. Still strokes the line of the ball religiously … strictly adheres to the principle that any shot across the line is evil! Incapable of long innings as often takes risks by driving 'on the up' as physical condition and concentration deteriorate. Loves bowling … particularly to 'Jono'. Wheels down his variations of leg spin, wrong-uns and flippers with a variety of actions. Great mimic. Favours a version of the Richie Benaud side-on at release glide … but occasionally will embark on a spell of 'Abdul Qadirs' where his flailing arms and heavily spun googly do the Pakistani little justice. Valiantly tries to hit the grease patch with his flipper … lethal if it strikes oil, sits up and begs a boundary if it doesn't. Better with an old tennis ball … gets more pace off the deck with a hairless rock.

After five or so years of battle on the carport concrete and with honours about even, it was unanimously decided by all four players that a Super Test be played to decide, once and for all, the champion team. Besides, the three teenagers had driver's licences and, I sensed, it was becoming less 'cool' to be seen playing cricket with a tennis ball and Sulo bins.

Saturday November 5, 2005, was to be the day.

Late afternoon the match began. Dan won the toss and sent us in – my creaking 1978 Mercedes car had had a particularly bad night and there was fresh oil on the grease patch.

Tom opened the batting. At once, he was away … hitting regular straight fours and sixes. Dan always searched for the Yorker against him or tried to sneak one between bat and pad when bowling his off breaks. Tom might be stiff legged at the crease but he has the eye of a dead fish and the ball was finding the middle of his flashing blade. He was particularly savage on Jono because he was slower than Dan and more 'sloggable'. Having raced to a half century he flashed at a quicker off break from Dan and edged to the automatic 'wicky' for a sparkling 64.

I started slowly. A signature boringly mistake-free dig was required. This was a 150 plus pitch. Jono got me to fizz off the grease patch and an lbw decision was debated. I reasoned that it was missing leg ... reluctantly Dan and Jono agreed. It's sometimes good to have influence through age. I began to strike regular fours as Dan dropped short ... by staying still and driving off the back foot down the line of the ball I was finding gaps between Jono at mid-on and Dan. Old fashioned cricket works ... ask Dizzy Gillespie after his double ton. At 44, I offered a simple caught and bowled and Jono snaffled it at the third attempt.

They're chasing a first innings total of 108 and are immediately in trouble ... Tom yorks Dan and Jono is under pressure – I'm spinning it past his bat and the wrong-uns keep going between a yawning bat and pad gap. He's reduced to a prodding shell of a batsman. Now for the flipper ... it pitches ... strikes grease ... zoots ... and finds middle stump halfway up. On your bike, Jono! Jono and Dan have only managed 22 between them. Tom customarily suggests we should attack from the outset of our second innings and is lacing fours – four in succession off Jono before he tries once too often and is caught one-handed off the house wall.

Our lead is 110 and I'm at the crease … and pumped!! Neat forward defence shots for singles and the occasional thumping front foot off drive for four. Just like Dizzy. The lead is out to 145 when Dan gets one to bite and the bin at short leg takes me via the inside edge. They need 146 to be the all-time champions … Tom and I agree if we can get Dan early, the pressure on Jono facing my leg breaks will be too much for the gentle kid from Kogarah Bay. Dan is playing out of his fair skin, however. He's square cutting strongly – if you get it past the back steps where point would normally field, you get four. It's risky because any edge to the back wall is automatically out. Dan is pasting Tom's slower balls – they are 'tripe' and I'm wearing them on the back and the legs at short mid-on. Within ten minutes, Dan has raised his bat for a century – it is customary to acknowledge a milestone in our game so Tom and I give him a generous round of applause. The reality confronting us is that Dan is going to chase down 146 by himself … the tennis ball's hair has gone shaggy and there is no pace off the pitch as a consequence. We're staring down the gun barrel. On 130, Dan makes a mistake … he tries to drive my dipping 'Richie Benaud' leg break and edges to slip. Yes!!! Still 16 needed

and Jono to bat under all sorts of pressure. He's very nervous …
trying to let as many leg breaks go as he can … he's even letting
wrong-uns go but, to our frustration, they're bouncing over the
top of middle stump. Tom is tired … he's bowled valiantly in
stifling conditions. Jono somehow scrounges his way to 10 – they
now need six to win the Super Test. I begin a new over. I start
with two leg breaks which beat a hesitant bat. You can cut the air
with a knife … Tom is fairly phlegmatic but even he is groaning
at Jono's luck from mid-on. Third ball just has to be the flipper
… Jono would have known it's either going to be that skidder or
a wrong-un. I am at the top of my run-up. This is the ball which
will determine the bragging rights for years to come. It pitches
perfectly … right in the middle of the grease patch … and it's
shooting towards middle. Jono is at the top of his backlift … he's
smelt a rat … suddenly he quickens his downstroke … and goes
for glory. It's only a split second but I'm backing my flipper … but
… crash … it's launched over Tom's head and rising … over my
head and rising more! And out of the driveway … over the road
… it sails … high … handsome … and finally resting on the top
of our neighbour Wim Smit's carport. A strike of fifty yards. Jono
is the hero … Dan and he are high tenning. I can't believe it. I'm
stunned. Tom heads to the kitchen for a Mars Bar – that kid gets
over things very quickly. Dan and Jono are the champions.

That Jono straight drive haunts me every day as I reverse out of the drive because the tennis ball is still nestled squarely in the middle of Wim's carport roof. It will remain Jono Gardner's badge of honour forever. Great game, fellas!!

There has not been another game of carport cricket since that day … another chapter on fatherhood closes.

5 November 2005

Skull's Ashes Tour Diary: From Home

Tuesday

Still jetlagged four days after my return flight from London, I'm unable to sleep. It's 3.30 am … I'm listening to midnight-to-dawn talkback radio. It's the third night in a row – I feel like a regular. Think I'll ring the host to discuss why 'y' is the forgotten vowel or something as atom-splitting. Get out of bed at 5 am and ask if I can accompany my youngest son, Tom, to swimming training. He agrees but stipulates there be no conversation in the car. Fair enough at that hour.

We're at Carss Park Pool at 5.20 am and Dick Caine – a 43-year veteran coach – is barking warm-up instructions in the 4-degree morning. If Andrew Symonds was forced to train at swimmers' hours, he still be playing Test cricket. Caine passes a 13-year-old huddling under a trenchcoat, sitting numbly still gazing at the cold concrete. 'Ready to fire up?' Caine beams. The boy remains expressionless and does not answer. 'How do you cope with such enthusiasm, Dick?' I ask. 'You get used to it, mate,' he drolly remarks. Another day has started. All the cricket conjecture surrounds whether Mitchell Johnson will play the third test at Edgbaston … Michael Clarke says Mitch is bowling great … in the nets. Not that old chestnut!

Wednesday

Just the two hours sleep … how did Napoleon or Alan Jones manage on that amount of shut-eye? Will be returning to England next week for the Headingly Test … can't wait. Rang the 'Headingly Swing King' Gary 'Gus' Gilmour to see how his health is going with his new liver. Think I need a new body clock. 'Gus' is in Newcastle, working at the John Hunter Hospital and getting on with his life. At his prime with a Duke ball in his hand and heavy cloud cover, 'Gus' swung it more than Benny Goodman.

Little Justin Langer is reported to have said he'd be available to open the innings if diminutive Phil Hughes is in trouble … he's supposed to be mentoring him, not replacing him! Ian Bell will bat four for England tomorrow … good! 'Belly' reminds me of former England middle order man Keith Fletcher, who used to prepare for his tilts with the great Dennis Lillee by practising taking off his pads!!

Thursday

It's been raining heavily at Edgbaston. I'm watching the SBS coverage of the first day. Stuart MacGill is a very promising talent … in time the former leg spinner will be a media star! Greg 'Mo' Matthews loves cricket more than any man in the country – his intuitive, straightforward thoughts on the game make good viewing. 'Mo' may not be in the frame to take the beige of Richie Benaud, but his insights have hopefully found a niche on SBS.

Shane Watson will open the batting instead of Hughes and Johnson is retained. The team balance is all about accommodating Mitch, who, we're told, won't be taking the new ball. If that tactic doesn't work out, in the next Test Johnson will be bowling left-arm Chinamen and Simon Katich will be opening the batting and the bowling. It appears that Stuart Clark is like cauliflower at buffets … extremely good for you but often rejected!

Play begins and Watson is immediately impressive. The general opinion seems to be that the burly Queenslander is better suited at number six … I disagree completely. Watson reminds me a lot of the great Michael Slater – technically pure and powerful;

an opener who takes time to find his rhythm against the new ball and then hurt the old. Plus he has now added a powerful square cut to his repertoire. 'Watto', too, has had problems with spinners' variations over the years – recently Pakistan off spinner Saeed Ajmal confused the blonde in Dubai with his doosra so much that instead of calling for new gloves at a break, he should have requested a dog and white stick.

Friday

I'm hosting my son Daniel's 21st birthday party at an inner city hotel and trying to watch the Australian batting on the big screen – it's difficult!! I can't hear any commentary because Swedish heavy metal group Soilworks is pounding my eardrums. Aren't all Swedes supposed to be quiet like Mats Wilander? James Anderson appears to be swinging it both ways – delivering more ins and outs than a cabinet reshuffle. Why can't we swing it like that? Otis Gibson, the England bowling coach, leads Troy Cooley by a long way so far this series. Australia is all out for 263 and Andrew Strauss is again hurting us with his square of the wicket game. Suddenly Bell is trapped dead in front by Johnson … except Rudi Koertzen rules not out. Fair dinkum, are Rudi and Mitch's mum in cahoots? Finally, Soilworks run out of grunt and I can go home to two hours sleep. See you from Headingly.

Wednesday

Economy air travel is everything it's supposed to be – economy of space … economy of love … the stewardesses have noticed that I'm an uncomfortable traveller. I think what gave it away was that I'm drinking my coffee in the brace position. A comforting flight attendant has informed me that air turbulence is just like riding a large boat over waves – nothing to worry about. Maybe someone should have assured Gene Hackman that when he was aboard the *Poseidon*. We're over the Bay of Bengal – a notoriously turbulent zone – everyone is calm except me. The last time I experienced wind like that was when I walked past Warney's room after his baked-bean breakfast. I'm talking nonstop to the French backpacker next to me … I'm sure he's thinking about how much it would cost to escape to business class.

How did Australian cricket teams in the bad old days survive economy travel on this long flight to England? Poor old Bruce Reid, at 6 foot 10 and with a chronic back problem he must have struggled in 85F. The cricket talk on arrival is about Stuart Clark perhaps making the starting eleven for Leeds … he should be a shoo-in. Peter Siddle could be the fall guy. The Victorian paceman has tried too hard to be Merv Hughes when I reckon he's better suited to being Paul Reiffel. The draw at Edgbaston highlighted the maturity of Michael Clarke – 'Pup' smelled the ball from the outset, batted behind his left shoulder and took his team out of a jam. Despite the trappings of wealth and high profile, 'Pup's' main priority is undoubtedly to contribute to an Australian cricket supremacy.

Thursday

I was last in Leeds in 1977 but certain aspects of this Yorkshire city haven't changed one bit. For starters its rugby league team is still among the most powerful in Great Britain and pay the best, while Leeds provides the most generous mugs for your tea in hotel rooms. Synchronised swimmers could train in them they're that big. Enough of the pluses: Leeds is a dour, grey collection of morbid buildings with a complex road system designed by the same guy who did Sydney. Around its CBD, satellite navigation sets regularly sigh, 'Stoofed if I know, old cock.'

I'm hosting 70 Australian supporters for the fourth and fifth Tests at the Oval. Neil and Mary Holton – two long-serving Woodville (Adelaide) Cricket Club officials are with me again. They did a Brian Goorjian: turning wooden-spooners into back-to-back A-grade premiers over the last three years. Andrew Doyle is a 180-kilo real estate agent from Alice Springs who only drinks spirits because he doesn't want to put on weight. My group will be sitting in the Western Stand tomorrow … it is the area with a bad reputation for misbehaviour and will be closely monitored by ground security. I have warned gentle 86-year-old Arthur Purvis – a 40-year club veteran with Petersham – that any untoward gesture during play and he'll be playing bingo for the rest of the Test. On the eve of the match, Ricky Ponting is saying at a press conference that it doesn't concern him that the crowd boos him when he walks out to bat – good onya, Snidely Whiplash! Australia may be considering Brett Lee and Stuart Clark for this must-win game – Lee wants to play but has patchy first-up form and Clark is surprisingly perceived as operating slower than Cliff Young.

Friday

Our hotel is just across the road from the Tetley's Brewery and the fumes are suffocating … two teetotallers in the group went for an early morning power walk and came back slurring their words. Suddenly I'm seated in the stands and Andrew Strauss has won the toss and elected to bat. Just after lunch the Poms finish batting – all out for 102! Siddle bowls like Reiffel, Stuart Clark sheds the Cliff Young tag and bowls like McGrath and the slips catch everything but swine flu. The English batsmen choose to play poor line … they kept playing down the Illawarra – should have been on the East Hills! Next minute born-again opener

Shane Watson is attacking from the outset and Ricky Ponting is giving a masterclass on back-foot batsmanship.

I'm sitting next to the identical Walder twins – Jim and Bob. They are the purest of cricket tragic, born an hour apart, who live together in Burmein just out of Mildura and get up at 4 am a few times a week to drive a compaction truck to Western Australia and back. All the time talking cricket!

The Pommy fast bowlers are bowling shorter than Danny de Vito and are getting cut and pulled to all parts. 'Mr Cricket' Mike Hussey fails again and his average has plummeted to 52 – he'd be captain coach of England if he'd owned a corgi. Mick Clarke is again being worked over by the thuggish English bowlers but survives till stumps. Both umpires have contacted Rudi Koertzen for advice on the preferred colour of seeing-eye dogs. Yorkshire supporters are shouting at us that we should go back to jail and chanting: 'If you're leading 1–0 stand up!' By Monday afternoon we'll be going with 'You're not singing anymore!'

Sunday

After the Headingley fourth Test triumph inside three days, my tour group has travelled to Turkey for our Gallipoli experience. Today we are in Istanbul and visiting the Grand Bazaar – a kilometre-long shopping arcade that makes Westfield Miranda look like the general store in Merriwa. There are thousands of locals selling carpets or jewellery. Most Turks seem to spend a great deal of time drinking reddish tea and smoking cigarettes. From what I saw, Doug Walters would be regarded as a social smoker in this country. At the World Athletics titles in Berlin, the Turkish 100-metre sprinter reportedly requested a smoking lane for his heat.

Monday

Another bucket list item has been ticked off. I am standing on the beach at Anzac Cove gazing up to the hills of Gallipoli. It is a solemn moment for all 70 Aussie tourists. Two things strike you about that fateful 1915 landing: the smallness of the beach area and how huge an advantage was the higher ground. My dear late father was a Changi POW whose wartime experience severely affected him reaching his full potential. Vera Rothwell from the Central Coast reads a moving ode to her Anzac grandfather and is roundly applauded by everybody. After a four-hour tour we travel by ferry to Çanakkale, where several toasts are made to the fallen throughout a long night of respectful celebration.

Wednesday

I'm having a pint or two at the Lord's Tavern after the obligatory tour of cricket's headquarters. My company includes Andrew

Doyle, a real estate agent from Alice Springs, and Brendan Eames, a trade union official from Melbourne – this is a shout of W. S. Cox Plate standard and, these days, I'm looking for soft winds at picnic meetings. Nonetheless, I'm holding my own.

The Tavern has changed – it is not the steeped-in-tradition cricket pub I once knew. It is now a brasserie with a polished timber floor … gone are the low ceilings, the stained carpet and the damp smell. Time waits for nobody.

On the television monitor we see Andrew Flintoff, who will play at the Oval tomorrow in white boots and with injections into his knee. We all agree that Changa Langlands in 1975 had those same good intentions. It's getting late. All three Aussie 400-metre male runners are bundled out in the semi-finals at the World Titles. Bring back Percy Cerutty, we chorus! I told you it was late. Then we're told the 18-year-old South African girl who we watch win the women's 800-metre final is supposed to be a bloke. Time, gentlemen, please.

Thursday

The Fifth and deciding Test starts today. I can't sleep. I'm awake at 3 am listening to a radio station known as Mellow Magic. All the songs are … well … mellow! I reckon hospitals should use the Carpenters' albums as general anaesthetic. I drift into a deep sleep and then I'm in the Laker Stand at the Oval awaiting the start of play. The Poms have allowed the pitch to bake uncovered throughout the previous day and the strip is as dry as Wayne Bennett. Against all rationale we still leave out the specialist spinner and England, who reportedly wanted to play two tweakers, lose their bottle and only Graeme Swann makes the eleven. Andrew Strauss wins a good toss and the ball disturbs the surface regularly throughout the day. We yield several wides and no balls. Only Kyle Sandilands oversteps the mark more than Mitchell Johnson. Peter Siddle bowls like John Snow to finish with four wickets. I'm sitting next to Ric Evans, a pleasant Western Australian, who umpired three tests in the 1980s. He reckons Swann will match Jim Laker and take 19 wickets in the match. At stumps on day one honours are even.

Friday

England has one hand on the Ashes – 15 wickets fell on an extraordinary second day. Pitches on which 15 or more wickets fall in a day are reported to the ECB. The Poms wanted a result and they will certainly get that. On the morning of the first day the Australian engine room think tank saw this Oval pitch as 'a second day Gabba strip and as hard as a rock'. Therefore, Stuart Clark was preferred to Nathan Hauritz. Unfortunately the ball was bursting through the top of the pitch within the first hour of play and is now turning like a top. It may prove a costly misread. At stumps England leads by 230 with seven wickets in hand. If 'Mr Cricket' Mike Hussey fails in the second innings he'll be 'Mr State Cricket' in October. Careers are now on the line. Where's Warney?

2 August 2009

Shock Jock

At dinner on Thursday night my sons accused me of trying to be a 'shock jock' when I casually mentioned that I thought the West Indies were a genuine chance at $11 to beat Australia in the First Test at the Gabba in ten days' time. Accusations of being un-Australian were hurled across the table. Look, I'm as Aussie as … I mean, I've booed politicians at sporting events and I start reading the paper from the back. But I'm also awake to a beatable odds-on favourite … and that could well be Ricky Ponting's Test team.

There is the quick adjustment time, for starters. The Australians have spent a month in India on pitches slower than Forrest Gump and arrive at a Gabba strip that could rival Dolly Parton for bounce. All the talk out of the camp is of one-day triumphs. The bottom line is that this winter the boys lost the

Ashes! Ponting has committed Australian cricket's mortal sin ... again. Beating India in a meaningless limited-over series soon after the Ashes calamity is a little like crashing out in the first round of the Wimbledon singles but winning the mixed doubles.

Quite frankly, Australia needs an early Test kill this summer and while Chris Gayle's West Indians might appear vulnerable, they could well be very dangerous. Their pace quartet of Jerome Taylor, Kemar Roach, Gavin Tonge and Dwayne Bravo screams potential to take 20 wickets on the right surface. Okay, the selectors should have included Usain Bolt on the form I saw on cable television a few weeks ago. In a charity match, Bolt took out Gayle's off pole with a Curtley Ambrose-like yorker then smashed 13 runs off 10 deliveries before being run out attempting a fifth ... to mid-off!!

Seriously, though, the big moment in Brisbane could be the Jerome Taylor opening spell to Ponting. There will be smart money on the Taylor off-cutter to knock over the Aussie captain yet again. Taylor has something of a grip on 'Punter', having dismissed him nine times in 11 international matches – five of which were lbw decisions. That sort of statistic is harder to ignore than a Bart Cummings eyebrow. On that subject, I would pay good money to watch Bart's 'brow take on one of John Howard's over three one-minute frowns.

The other pacemen, Roach and Tonge, bowl genuine outswingers to right handers and maintain consistent lines. If both find the right length at the Gabba, look out!

Gayle, of course, has to switch on – given that his normal state is close to comatose, the West Indies skipper has to give his team the impression that he is as excited about Test cricket as Big Kev!

From the Australian viewpoint, I would play Brett Lee in a heartbeat. If 'Binga' can get through the next few days cricket for New South Wales and pull up strongly, he should be in a four-pronged pace attack in Brisbane. After such a devastating loss at the Oval last August, there are usually casualties. Sadly, Stuie Clark looks as contemporary as a skivvy these days, while Nathan Hauritz – unwisely left out of that game – seems to be trusted as much as Hannibal Lecter on tuck shop duty. Lee looks the perfect replacement for either. I can't recall a cricketer in recent times who has polarised opinion as much as the blond paceman. The majority believe his 300-plus Test wicket haul is fully justified, but, curiously, there are sections who see him as an overrated pretty boy who has started that lawn mower once too often. Lee has a lot of Justin Langer in him – he is driven to prove his critics wrong. He's a fighter who relishes returning from setbacks to succeed. There is also the small matter of the veteran paceman having a stunning record against the Windies big guns

Gayle and Ramnaresh Sarwan. Lee has snared Gayle ten times in 26 internationals and Sarwan an incredible 15 in 29 contests. To leave a fully fit Lee out of the Gabba squad would be yet another selection clanger!

15 November 2009

Everything to McGain

Bryce McGain looks more like Hugh Grant than Hugh Grant, and is reportedly just as vague. I mean, this is the fellow who on being selected to represent Australia promptly missed his plane to South Africa and then was allegedly late for the team bus on a match day. To compound these indiscretions he returned 0–149 at Capetown in his solitary test … and he's 37! Why am I even writing about him, you say?

Well, for starters the Victorian leg spinner is the most potent striker amongst the slow bowlers in our domestic cricket and I have just finished watching him fizz some really good stuff this week at the Melbourne Cricket Ground, taking a match-winning seven-wicket haul against Western Australia. Were he to retain that zip over the next month and Nathan Hauritz not contribute strongly against the West Indies, I would select McGain to play against the Pakistanis on Boxing Day in Melbourne. This fellow is a real horses-for-courses proposition. He is as good a bet as Robert 'Dutchy' Holland was at 38. Even the great Shane Warne was moved to text a message of support after his Capetown meltdown. If 'Warney' sends you a text and you're male … you've got something!

Warne recognised that McGain was returning too early after shoulder surgery; was under-done. To boot, he was condemned to bowl to in-form batsmen AB de Villiers and Ashwell Prince to a curious and unforgiving field. Even the master might have struggled in such circumstances. Wrist spinners have to be cuddled … and encouraged. McGain was seemingly shown no love and the door almost simultaneously.

I am at my wits' end pondering why our selectors are consumed with off spinners anyway. All the talk for the spin spot in our Test team is of Hauritz or Jason Krejza. Please list me the matches these two have won for their respective states. It's un-Australian to field an Aussie test team without a 'wristy'. Would you make an Australian chick flick with Bill Hunter as the romantic lead? I don't think so! Finger spinners like to count leg spinners as brothers … they're not our brothers … they are distant cousins who have taken the soft option! When you've exhausted all other bowling alternatives with little success ... you try off spin. It is the breaststroke of cricket.

Andrew Hilditch is talking long-term policies and the Ashes next November. What about the short term and the winning of Test matches over the next couple of months against teams like Pakistan and New Zealand, who historically regard leg spin as extra-terrestrial? Warne filled his boots against these two nations ... even I looked forward to playing them. It is my judgment that Pakistanis and Kiwis seem to regard the leg spinner as a mystery ball: something of an over-read, to be frank.

The first two Tests against Pakistan are in Melbourne and Sydney from Boxing Day. McGain's combined statistics at these venues are undeniable. In State games over the last couple of years, McGain has taken 53 wickets at about 29 runs each; in contrast, Hauritz has taken 27 wickets at 49 runs apiece. Logic would suggest McGain is more likely to win a Test match on the last day at the MCG or SCG than any other slow man in the country. Of course, he's too old ... absolutely, he's not the future. But shouldn't we be thinking of the present – winning the Test match in front of us would be nice. If McGain had played at the Oval last August, we'd hold the Ashes.

Victoria wins matches in all three forms of the game with McGain in the eleven. It is whispered his tour report card after

South Africa was not complimentary and that he failed to win the full endorsement of Ricky Ponting. In most eras that would mean the end; these times, however, are particular circumstances where Australia is searching for a spinner capable of making deep incisions into a batting line up. Australia tends to look to fast men Mitchell Johnson and Peter Siddle to win matches on wearing last day pitches – 'Hugh' McGain should be re-entertained … 'one Test wonder' is not a fitting epitaph for his gift.

22 November 2009

The Walkerville Lawn Tennis Title

It's the Sunday of the Australia Day long weekend … I'm in Adelaide to cover the one day internationals matches involving Australia and Zimbabwe.

I have deliberately kept myself tidy for today as I have a physical challenge ahead. This afternoon the Walkerville Tennis Open will be held at Jack & Sue Clarke's house in the leafy northern Adelaide suburb of Walkerville. Jack is a board member of Cricket Australia, a partner in a leading law firm and the best judge of wine in the whole of South Australia. His Australia Day weekend barbecue has developed a reputation akin to the Tour de France – it is the survival of the fittest. His stately Federation home boasts a lawn tennis court and all the invited guests who fancy themselves at this ancient game have been invited to bring a racquet.

Some real power players of Australian cricket have been summoned … Bob Merriman and Creagh O'Connor will be there representing Cricket Australia … the former West Indian great Clive Lloyd will attend and it will be good to see big 'Hubert' a gentle man who oversaw the most vindictive period of concentrated fast bowling in West Indian cricket history. A number of Channel 9 commentary team will be there, notably Ian Healy, Mark Taylor and Simon O'Donnell.

I have no serious claims as a tennis player but I have been having a practice hit regularly with my son Daniel over the last few months and have been showing reasonable form on synthetic surfaces. The well-manicured grass of Walkerville will be different altogether.

I arrive at the Clarkes around 2 o'clock … under my arm are my Bjorn Borg wooden racquet and two bottles of the most expensive red I could summon at a nearby liquor outlet. Jack greets me warmly at the door, takes my wine, inspects the brand and announces to Sue that 'Skull has bought some stuff that will go well in cooking'. He's such a wine snob! Other guests arrive in dribs and drabs … some have bought a racquet, others will borrow from the Clarke collection.

There is no warm-up period when you attend a Jack Clarke barbecue ... two dozen bottles of his finest read have been opened and are airing close to where the sausages are sizzling and guests are already strongly imbibing with unbridled enthusiasm. People are paddling up and down and doing awful belly flops ... I'm drinking soda water ... there is much to accomplish in just a while.

Jack bellows that the tennis should begin and initially it's just a few sets of friendly doubles ... that suits me ... I'm getting a good feel for the court surface. My forehand cross court is going well and will be a weapon at the business end of the day. Enough of the doubles – we need an overall singles winner, Jack announces. It is down to a field of four ... Healy the Queenslander whose deft touches at the net appear his strength but who is inconsistent and makes numerous unforced errors with his forehand ... Taylor, who emerged from Wagga Wagga as an Australian Rules footballer and cricketer but who on the evidence of his service action thought a racquet was something which involved Al Capone ... the dark horse, quite obviously, is the Victorian O'Donnell – strong and well co-ordinated, the former all rounder came out of Assumption College, Kilmore, with a background in Australian Rules, cricket and whatever else he turned his hand to ... 'Scoob' is going to be hard to beat.

With just four entrants we're already at the semi-final stage and at once Healy and O'Donnell are locked in battle. The Victorian's strength is built around his serve volley game and he duly trounces the error-prone Healy 12–5. It was decided to play every serve as a point and the first to 12 with an advantage of two would go through to the final. Healy takes his loss philosophically and seeks consolation in a vat of the Barossa Valley's finest.

I'm up against Taylor ... 'Tubby' could catch butterflies at first slip but his work on the grass with his big booming aluminium racquet leaves a lot to be desired ... I'm waltzing him around the court, working him hard from left to right but, moreover, I'm monstering his serve ... in a short space of time I've recorded at 12–4 victory.

The final is up immediately ... my opponent O'Donnell downs a beer – I decline. I'm ready for this big Victorian. The match gets underway without too much audience attention although there is the odd chair that has been turned around to enjoy this classic battle between the younger O'Donnell and the wily leg-spinning veteran. O'Donnell's game is as expected, all about hustle and bustle, serving strongly and charging the net ... to beat him I'll need my passing shots to work. The score has reached four ... I'm making too many errors ... his power game is threatening to crush me ... I'm playing a lot of Lleyton

Hewitt type rallies – defending strongly but never hitting with a strength to pass the incredible wing span of the former St Kilda forward … at eight all it looks as if it's going to go to the wire but suddenly there is a chink in the O'Donnell armour. His backhand, which has held up pretty well under his net challenges, has suddenly started to look a little ragged the more ground he is forced to cover. I start to direct all my shots to his backhand … three times in a row he nets and the other he hits wide of the baseline … I lead 11–9 … I need just one good serve … it's to the forehand court … he gets it back … I stay on the baseline … I'm saying to myself, 'No errors here Skull, the cup is yours with one O'Donnell error.' He's still in the point, the rally has gone for close to 20 shots … he pops one high back over the net … I should have smashed it away but decide to play the percentages and keep it in play … he lobs me … I chase back, turn … I need a clear winner … my forehand cross court just has to be the cup-winning stroke … it beats O'Donnell's lunge at the net, catches the line and I've won 12–9. Simon is gracious in defeat and shakes my hand warmly at the net.

For the next two hours I was crushingly boring … talking anybody who wants to listen through my triumph, how much I prepared, how badly I wanted it … it means nothing to any of them … nobody knew that I'd taken it this seriously … this was

ABC v. Channel 9 – it was personal. I was defending 'Aunty'. The sausages are sizzling and the best of the Barossa's wines are being drunk at a rapid rate. Guests are starting to fall like flies … I'm telling board chairman, Bob Merriman, what was wrong with cricket administration in the '70s – he's probably heard it all before. Clive Lloyd is seeking Jack's counsel … but doesn't seem to be understanding the host's rationale.

It's now 2 am and the discussion is all about the wealthiest cricketer of our eras … I've volunteered Dennis Lillee … Healy says that he'll see my Lillee and raise me a Mark Taylor.

In a twinkling it's 3 am – there's only Jack and me left. The barbecue has been turned off. 'Skull there's a bed inside for you if you'd like to kip the night,' the host kindly offers. 'I'll be there in a minute,' I volunteer. Then I began a belated walk across the tennis court, the scene of my triumph some 11 hours earlier. Suddenly I hit the net and trip … getting up was going to be very difficult so I grabbed a cushion off a nearby chair – it was to be my pillow for the night … I curled up just inside the backhand service box and slept the sleep of a winner.

At 6 am I was woken by water … it wasn't rain … it was Jack's sprinklers going off … I was a foot from them … I thought somebody was tipping a bucket of water over me … I'm drenched. I've got my wooden racquet, my dignity and nothing much else.

I walk out on to the streets of Walkerville. A cab somehow picks me up despite the state I'm in. I sit in the backseat and explain that I've slept on a sprinkler. Back at the hotel I need better sleep. I rest till midday.

My ABC colleague, Jim Maxwell, knocks on the door: 'Are you ready to go to the ground?' I said, 'Damn straight,' although I'm far from ready. The commentary that afternoon was as good as I could manage in my state … I could barely see … adjectives were kept to a minimum … the piece of cricket was either good or bad … nothing deeper than that … apparently the professionalism at Channel 9 had also been compromised.

At sunset Jack Clarke appears at the back of the box; my host from the night before announces he has an envelope for me … I'm in the commentary chair at the time going live to the country … Jack announces, 'Your room key, sir,' and delivers the envelope. I open it … the contents are five blades of grass. Thank you, Jack. What a great host!

25 January 2004

Oh Captain, My Captain

In a perfect world all the speculation would surround who may succeed Shane Warne as Australian Test captain. Warney should have been our skipper for almost a decade except for … nightfall! Nonetheless, the great leg spinner has always endorsed Michael Clarke to succeed Ricky Ponting when Punter finally calls it a day. Apparently, Ponting still sees himself calling the toss at Lord's in 2013 … just as Richie Benaud will probably hand over the beige to Michael Slater's son in a couple of decades, this saga is far from over.

For starters, there is Clarke's back: Quasimodo has reportedly seen 'Pup's' spinal x-rays and feels better about himself. And there is the small matter of public opinion. Recently voted our most overrated cricketer, a majority seem to believe Clarke has caught far too many tennis balls in his jocks and would have been better off buying his chick a Morris Oxford instead of an Aston Martin. As well, the moniker 'Pup' has to go. It is just not a great sit. I mean, there are not too many heart surgeons out there who are comfortable with being nicknamed 'Clumsy'.

Rightly or wrongly, image counts. For instance, Shane Watson is seen as lucky and far too gorgeous while Brad Hodge is regarded as a cuddly, hard-done-by battler. To the general public, Simon Katich has been an underrated good bloke throughout his whole career as well as somebody who advises Wolverine on how to live with excessive body hair. On that matter, Doug Bollinger – whose rug, sadly, is noticeably thinning – should seek a transplant from Kat's chest. Fair dinkum, that foliage could take root on Peter Garret's melon!

But back to Clarke and his test captaincy aspirations. For starters, I would immediately relieve him of the Twenty20 leadership. Frankly, 'Pup's' batting is not built for helter-skelter – his strike rate is lower than a panda's libido and he simply does not have the strength to hit enough sixes. Olive Oyl would fancy her chances in an arm wrestle against 'Pup'. My perfect Australian Twenty20 team would see Cameron White as skipper, Adam Gilchrist opening the batting, Hodge at number three, Glenn McGrath with the new rock and Warney as coach/manager. Yes, I'm trapped in a time warp.

However, from a Test viewpoint, Clarke's main objective over the next few years must be to concentrate on winning the dressing room and working on his presence – there is a strong similarity between 'Pup' and Kim Hughes. There was much more to Hughes than his emotional resignation but the man in the street seems to identify him only with the tears. Had the

Western Australian not coveted the captaincy, I'm convinced he would have averaged around 50 in Test cricket and been regarded as one of our best ever batsmen. Kim possessed all the traits of the long-term lieutenant: committed, loyal and enthusiastic, but lacking the qualities to justify higher office. Promotion hurt him badly. Clarke and Hughes love and respect 'the cap' and those who serve with distinction under it. A few years back, when Brad Hogg announced his retirement from international cricket, Clarke took it upon himself to have a gold pen engraved to mark Hogg's contribution. 'Pup' presented it to him privately without fuss or fanfare. Here was a player building a platform discreetly but intentionally. 'Pup' Clarke may want the Test captaincy too much … just as Hughes found, it brings burdens that can break a man. Warney is his mentor, so tactical nous will not be an issue – presence and a dodgy back could be!

29 November 2009

More Breezies than Windies

Sadly, the West Indies are not what they were! Quite frankly, Chris Gayle's boys are just not physically intimidating – Mr Bean would fancy his chances of getting their play-lunch money in a schoolyard. Plus, they are the Fleetwood Mac of cricket – wracked by internal squabbling but with a groovy front person and still getting gigs around the world. The simple fact is that their only 6' 10" guy bowls slow finger spin, one of their opening bowlers is a chubby chops called Ravi and their key middle order batsman is little Brendan from Brisbane. These calypso kids are just not scary!!

Back in my day in the late '70s, when I was called off the bench to open the batting for the World Series Cricket cavaliers against

Clive Lloyd's team, I would regularly fill my jocks! That mob was frightening. My regular opening partner against Andy Roberts, Michael Holding and company was gentle Rick McCosker from Inverell. He was variously known as 'Rick the Rock' when batting well and 'Rick the Snick' when in a drought. I still have nightmares about a match in outback Traralgon, Victoria, when we were sent in on what looked a beast of a pitch. How did I know that it would behave worse than Oasis? Well, for starters, don't worry about a key: Tony Greig would have fallen down the cracks on a good length.

NOW IT'S OVER TO TONY FOR THE PITCH REPORT...

Asked to bat first, Rick took strike. Why? Because as we walked on to the ground I ran at full speed to the non striker's end and sat down! Bravely, Rick managed three boundaries over the slips heads in Roberts' first over. Before I faced a ball from Holding, I asked Rick to signal to our skipper Eddie Barlow that he should declare because we had enough runs! Rick, ever the conservative, suggested we may need a few more ... well, HE WASN'T FACING! My first delivery from Holding leapt from two feet outside off stump to strike me on the left shoulder: this was an accurate jaffa, given I was standing two feet outside leg stump at point of contact. Technically it was an off-cutter because it nearly cut off my head. My mind was not right. I flirted with asking Lloyd if I could retire hurt with chest pains but I didn't think he'd buy it.

The next ball was full ... I went half forward – make that quarter forward – only for this cobra to leap vertically at my gloves and fly straight up in the air. Before anybody could scream, I yelled, 'Catch it!' My innings was over – but I was alive. They were the Windies' glory days ... I would face this current pace attack wearing Tony Abbott's budgie smugglers and Danny Green's thongs! Okay, maybe I'd use a pad – but only one! It's amazing how brave you become in the commentary box.

It has not been a great week. Every Tuesday I take my beloved wife to the movies – we hold hands and do coffee. This week we went to the Dendy in crowded Newtown where you generally have to add the parking fine to the cost of the movie and choc top. My choice was *A Serious Man* – a Coen brothers production with rave reviews. Having seen *No Country for Old Men* I thought these outstanding Coens are great at murder and mayhem, why not comedy? Well ... I tried to walk out twice but my wife kept asking for a referral and somehow the decision was overturned! Fair dinkum, it reminded me of when Craig McLachlan attempted comedy on the *Footy Show* ... humour is not the Coens' bag!

My week worsened. On Wednesday night, hypnotised by Roy Jones Jr's record, I backed him at $3.50 to knock out Danny Green inside 12 rounds. Badly wrong within two minutes, I was heckled and jeered to bed by my sons for being unpatriotic and a turncoat. Green is a wonderful Australian and I had backed him to lose. I felt cheap, dirty ... I stood in the shower for 15 minutes – if Norman from *Psycho* had entered the ensuite with a knife, I'd have helped him pull back the shower curtain.

A day or so later I'm at the Adelaide Oval and front man Gayle has played an irresponsible shot and is out. Stevie Nicks' game is in better order at the moment.

6 December 2009

Up-and-Comers

Every December I take my family to Queensland's Noosa Heads for our annual holiday. We choose the Sunshine Coast above the Gold Coast for a couple of reasons. For a start there are no toolies arguing about their backpacker hostel bill on Hastings Street and, as well, Warwick Capper's meter maids have never quite cut the mustard with the Noosa Council. Communication with the locals is easy … you just add 'aye' at the end of every sentence. It's a cinch … aye!

Tonight we have pre-dinner drinks at a fashionable bar. Our cocktail waitress is young and very attractive … I keep thinking that my wish is that she will not soon bring up Tiger Woods' half century.

The draw in the Adelaide Test is hopefully memorable for the beginning of the demise of the referral system. When our game gets to the stage of backyard cricket, where batsmen refuse to take their dismissal like men, then we are in a grave state. If common sense rules, once the trial period is over the law makers will unanimously agree that the decision to go upstairs is exclusively with the umpire alone … as it is with referees in the NRL.

Another positive to come out of Adelaide was the obvious advances made by Doug Bollinger and Shane Watson in reverse-swinging the old ball. When Australia play Test series on the subcontinent next (hopefully in my lifetime), fast bowlers who can change the path of a soft blob of red cloth late in its path will be gold!

Watching New South Wales play Queensland in a 50-over match during the week, I reckon I saw Australia's own Javed Miandad batting for the Blues. Steven Smith strode out to bat at 4–78 in pursuit of 259 with the ball swinging more than George Michael. Smith was more Javed than Javed … though I suspect he wasn't trying to sell his match shirt on eBay at the dinner break. The 20-year-old Sutherland junior's game plan was simple: he kept out the brutes and dispatched the filth! Smith and Cyclops share a trait – both have a great eye! The aforementioned Smith is 'cricket smart' in a Javed way – he knew exactly how to get his team to the target and was still there on 75 not out when victory was completed.

Much has been made of Smith's talent as a leg spinner … despite having a bowling action looser than Paris Hilton. This point must be made – the Blues prodigy is a batsman first, and a slow bowler second. His passage to a baggy green cap should initially, however, be via the upcoming one-day series against the West Indies and Pakistan. Andrew Hilditch and company must include the youngster in the 50-over and Twenty20 squads at once: Smith is a better all-round option than either Adam Voges or Cameron White – he could easily be as effective as Pakistan's Shahid Afridi in the short-form games.

And, while they're at it, the national selectors could add New South Wales fast bowling prodigy Josh Hazlewood to the Test squad for the Boxing Day Test against Pakistan. This column advocated that Hazlewood should have been taken on the Ashes tour this year instead of Brett Lee – the 18-year-old is ready for five-day cricket now! This fellow has a bowling trajectory that only the greats can boast. With Stuart Clark now out of the picture, how refreshing it would be for a teenage fast bowler to be given a Rocky Balboa-like opportunity. Hazlewood's progress is being slowed by the constant diet of limited-over matches that have been his season so far. The search for the next Warne is a work in progress … the search for the next McGrath could end next week: pick Hazlewood for the MCG Test … aye!

13 December 2009

'The Pub Comp'

At the beginning of the 1968/69 season I was quite content to play for St George on a Saturday and dream of winning a NSW cap at some stage over the next year or so.

In early October came a call from the public phone of the Kurrajong Hotel, Erskineville. Jack Bugg, the treasurer of the pub's cricket team, was calling to invite me to have a Sunday game with his team of public bar drinkers. They played in a small competition comprised of a number of traditional working-class inner city inns. Now Jack was a heavily tattooed battler with a heart of gold who loved cricket and a schooner. He disliked hotels like the White Horse at St Peters and the Camelia Grove at Newtown – the Kurrajong needed strengthening and the committee reckoned that a little bit of cash might persuade me to turn out with the boys. He was right!!

I was placed on an incentive contract – it was more of a handshake arrangement, to be honest – payment was to be made at the conclusion of each match. The deal was simple – I would earn fifty cents for every wicket ... $5.00 for a fifty ... $10.00 for a century. All 'pub comp' matches were held simultaneously on the expansive area of Tempe Reserve ... malthoid pitches set alongside the Cooks River and a couple of hefty slogs from Mascot airport. The standard of cricket was very modest – each team would provide a keg of beer for its supporters and, er, players, for that matter. Many of the pub's regular would drop in to have a few beers and support the local. Barmaids of one establishment, it was whispered, would offer favours for particularly good performances on the field. Call me mercenary, but I was content to play for the money. Each hotel boasted one or two 'imports' who were playing first eleven at district level but the tail usually stared at number five and fell away alarmingly. I loved to have the ball in my hand when the third drop batsman was strolling to the crease. It was also an advantage to bat first ... post a big total ... and let the Reschs or Tooheys do its stuff under an afternoon sun. Many of my opponents would take guard without batting gloves ... uncomfortably play and miss at the first delivery and then lift out the protector and throw it to the square leg umpire for safe keeping. I did not have the heart to pitch a sharp turning wrong'un at these poor fellows. With the sun setting, I was often filling my boots with 'fifty cent' victims.

One day, the Camelia Grove number eleven was stumbling out to bat in a sad state of intoxication. All I could see was 50 cents!! Suddenly, ten yards from the pitch, he collapsed! There he lay … incapable of anything … I asked treasurer Bigg if I could claim him as a victim – I was a desperate man! Jack told me where to get off … the match was declared over … and we all marched to the beer tent while the number eleven slept soundly out in the middle. As a penniless student, I used to rely on the Kurrajong Hotel money for my social life. Every Sunday I would get cashed up and drive from Tempe to Auburn Baseball Club disco in my $70.00 Morris Oxford car. There I would dance terribly, drink copiously and around midnight chant for the resident crooner Reg Norton to finish the evening with a brilliant rendition of 'You'll Never Walk Alone'. Every Monday morning I would wake up broke and hung over … and count the week down to pay day at the 'pub comp'.

It was hardly the stuff of a future captain of industry … but, hell, I couldn't see past the White Horse Hotel tailenders at that stage of my life.

Open Sesame

It has to be said, Shane Watson is an outstanding Test opening batsman. There are some out there – you know who you are – who thought 'Watto' was just a little too cosmetically perfect, a little too – say it – soft! That whenever the blond signalled to the dressing room while batting, you thought it was for facial moisturiser, not batting gloves. Many sneered at his Richard Wilkins hair. And there were the consistent injuries. People sniggered he could strain a groin applying hair gel!

However, Watson has won virtually all the doubters over with the quality of his batting against the new ball over the last six months. Sure there are no hundreds yet and, yes, he gets struck on the legs more than your average kick-boxer but, make no mistake, Watto is the real deal at number one. He could well be Australia's version of the great South African Barry Richards. There is still a genuine belief that his best position is at number six. You have to ask yourself, though, does he have the game for that spot? At the moment Watson keeps getting out when set against the moving older ball.

The best number sixes over the years have been square of the wicket players who murder spin on all pitches … Watson is neither the most convincing cutter nor sweeper in the Australian game. And would the big Queenslander monster clever spinners with well-disguised doosras on dusty subcontinental pitches? On the evidence so far, no! Going in first and striking the lines down the ground against a new ball coming onto the bat with the field up the bat ideally suits the Watson mechanics. I speak from personal experience, because you may remember my epic innings of 14 opening the batting for Australia in the second innings of the Centenary Test against England at the MCG in 1977. Thirty-odd years later, people still come up and remind me of the cameo. Oh shucks, it was nothing, I demur. My call to arms came because our regular opener, Rick McCosker, had his jaw broken in five places by Bob Willis in the first innings. Willis was not going to land one on my chin … not from where I was going to be playing him, anyway. And, of course, captain Greg Chappell had mused – a little like the Watson case – whether opening the innings would prevent me from providing him with 10 to 15 quality overs with the ball? Well, given that I had yet to provide that in 20-odd previous tests, I guess it wasn't such an issue! Heh heh!

Test openers should have their own club ... a secret handshake, a subtle wink to each other across a room that says 'you're one of us'. We're not middle order pansies, we are in the front line ... taking-head on all the enemy can throw at us. Sorry, I have gone a little overboard. Just like I did at Bexley Golf Club a year or so ago, when I finally brought my handicap down from 10 to nine. That afternoon, after suitable celebratory schooners, I suggested to various committee men that the club should have a 'Single Figures Bar' where the elite could drink amongst ourselves and not have to talk to 18-markers about their luckless putting or bad bunker lies! Derided by all, a few weeks later I was back to double figures and talking about missed putts and bunker lies to the few who cared to listen.

But I digress ... changes to the Australian batting order are imminent. Ricky Ponting is injured, Mick Clarke's back looks stiffer than a Malcolm Reilly coathanger, Mike Hussey is in the dimming twilight, and Marcus North may just be too one-dimensional. Many alternative names will be raised. One that won't come up is burly South Australian Mark Cosgrove. 'Cossy' is a tremendous talent who smacked a limited-over century this week at the MCG, which was the equal of Chris Gayle's Perth ton.

This fellow is perhaps the cleanest hitter in the country. Let's be frank, however: 'Cossy' is more than burly, he carries a few extra kilos … Okay, he's a chubby chops! I think he's a terrific talent who should have won more international caps … but for his look. What's the problem? People love a fatty boom-bah!

Look at the lack of public affection for skinny-minny Michael Clarke. Now, 'Cossy' will not be catching tennis balls in his kaftan anytime soon and maybe … just maybe … he needs a strong mentor. What about John Daly, who this week was offering Tiger Woods marriage advice? That's like getting fashion tips from Al Grassby. Cosgrove is a mixture of Arjuna Ranatunga and Lance Cairns … he can deftly late cut past first slip or slap one into a different electorate. Maybe a Test call-up is out of the question, but I'm willing 'Cossy' for many more hundreds this summer and consideration for a recall to the limited-over squads. His restoration would be a triumph for all those who regard a Tim Tam as broccoli!

20 December 2009

Christmas Cheer

Last Monday was a strange day. The headline screamed 'I Forgive You, Shane' and it wasn't even Warney's missus. All the talk was of 'Puff Daddy' (Chris Gayle) and Shane Watson and 'that' celebration. Can we move on, pets? But hats off to 'Puff'! With a naked disdain for Test cricket, Gayle drifted into Brisbane last month, all rock-star T-shirt and gold-studded sunglasses, and promptly failed – shouldering arms twice to modest inswingers in the Gabba test. Then, within three weeks, the West Indian skipper had won two man of the match awards plus man of the series and displayed class and extreme diplomacy under pressure that would have made Quentin Bryce envious.

Financially, Monday was good. I am part-owner of a big-hearted four-year-old mare named Skulla's Sister who won an 1100-metre sprint at Dubbo races in the early evening. Michael

Travers – an underestimated Western Districts hoop – rode her like Scobie Breasley to swoop home and get the lollies. Look, I'm not saying she's Sunline, but she could be better than Mustard … if she lives that long! It has to be said, you're not in country racing to make a big quid: after you win a race in the bush and when all the fees are taken out plus the prize money that goes to the other nine owners, you've got just enough for a Kelly Country suit. Still, it's that priceless thrill of the noble thoroughbred that you feed beating the others to the post: whether it's Randwick or a picnic meet at Trangie, it's hard to explain the feeling to non-racing people.

On Tuesday I was a guest coach at a holiday cricket clinic. When I was introduced to the group comprising mostly 9- to 13-year-olds, I swear they thought, 'Oh, so Uncle Fester does cricket, as well.' Only three of the 50 youngsters bowled respectable leg spinners – I don't think the next Warney was amongst them. He was probably back home, lying on the family couch eating pizza, smoking and texting.

New South Wales prodigies Josh Hazlewood and Usman Khawaja announced themselves as future Test players on Wednesday in a Ford Ranger Cup match against Victoria at the SCG. I was there for ABC Radio, broadcasting ball-by-ball to anybody who has a digital radio or cared to listen on the internet.

In other words, our audience was a nerd short of a quorum! Still, we saw the further rising of a teenage pace bowler surely destined for 300-plus Test wickets and the progression of Khawaja, bound within 18 months or so to be Australia's first capped Muslim.

Christmas Day was awesome! I managed six cakes of perfumed soap and a bottle of cologne – the soaps were individually wrapped so I would have a fair representation of presents under the tree. I'm sure my family loves me, nonetheless. There was vision on the evening news of the Australian captain, his wife and daughter enjoying a blissful photo opportunity at their five-star Melbourne hotel. Just one year, I would like to see one of the Aussie player's children chucking a tantrum or, even better, two fast bowlers walking past the Christmas tree holding hands.

I'm envious, too, of their hotel. I never played a Boxing Day Test, but for some years in the late '60s and early '70s, New South Wales would play Victoria in a Sheffield Shield match over that period – Christmas Day would be the rest day. We stayed in a 'quarter-star' pub on Flinders Street called Hosies. It was rough, to say the least. One year I asked the manager why the bar didn't have a bistro. 'Simple,' he told me. 'Our clientele would rather have a fight than a feed.' You can't argue with that sort of logic.

News comes out of Melbourne that Steven Smith has again joined the squad as cover for an injured Nathan Hauritz ... fair dinkum, in recent times 'Horrie' has been covered more than Amazing Grace. Mike Hussey's position is again being questioned – his big scores have dried up. I've counted more teeth on working-class Russians than 'Mr Cricket's' Test numbers in the last 12 months.

27 December 2009

Skull's Fountain of Youth

Forget Viagra or jumping into a swimming pool like those old fogies in *Cocoon*, if you want to get excited and stay young, just drive up and down Driver Avenue at Moore Park a couple of times a week. Of course, I can't speak for everybody, but I reckon watching Test cricket at the SCG is better than sex. I'm up for it once a year, anyway. SCG is the Cate Blanchett of cricket grounds – eternally dignified yet with dollops of sensuality and emotion. Okay … I'm in love with the joint! All right? I've been coming to the place for over 50 years and I'm here again this weekend. Every visit has provided a lasting memory. Here are a few:

7th Test 1971 v. England

This match was Ian Chappell's debut as Australian captain ... and we lost! I took my first Test wicket: if you can't start at the top you may as well start with ... Keith Fletcher! Who? Yes, 'Fletch' was a good little bloke – most of our team didn't like him because he retaliated when Dennis Lillee sledged him and was rumoured to have a great cricket brain. Unless you were Gary Sobers, these were mortal sins to our boys in the 70s. Anyway, 'Fletch' was batting away. I came on to bowl and served him up a juicy nude nut ... he naively played for spin and Keith Stackpole took the inside-edged catch at short leg. You never forget your first!

3rd Test 1992 v. India

Australia chose a modestly performed blond-headed leg spinner with muffin top hips and the gamble failed badly. And no, it wasn't me ... I mean, the selectors hadn't picked me for 15 years now, so I figured that I was part of an extended rotation policy. No ... this 'leggy' was called Shane Warne. His match figures were a shattering 1–150! I was doing some casual media work and wrote in my diary at the end of the match: 'Warne rolls out non-spinning leg breaks from a jerky, mechanically poor action. He is reasonably accurate but appears to rely too heavily on his wrong 'un, which seems easy to detect. His flipper is erratic. No future!

The selectors have got this one wrong!' All right, so I may have been slightly off the mark. Seven hundred and eight Test wickets off the mark, if you have to be pedantic!

3rd Test 1993 v. West Indies

Allan Border became the second batsman to score 10,000 Test runs when he made 74 in Australia's first innings. This is the same pugnacious little 'lefty' who emerged from North Sydney Boys' High with a limited stroke range and a rare gift. 'AB' just didn't get out! He practised not getting out! He rehearsed not making mistakes and keeping the ball on the ground with that paddlepop stick of a Duncan Fearnley bat … I don't know what 'AB' makes of the modern game. In this match, too, West Indies champion Brian Lara princed a brilliant 277 … it remains the best innings I have ever seen from the stands. Lara would have made at least 400 that day until tragically run out by team-mate Carl Hooper. Everybody at the ground felt cheated. For years I seriously thought of ringing Sydney talkback radio stations and whingeing about why Hooper wasn't jailed for his running between wickets.

5th Test 2003 v. England

When Steve Waugh strode out to bat shortly before tea on the second day, he was a dead man walking. If he nicked the first ball, I reckoned his Test career would be over. At that stage of his career 'Tugga's' body was held together by gaffer tape and the selectors had arranged for a gold watch to be engraved. With one ball to go in the day's play, Waugh was on 98. Only a handful of the 41,931 spectators had left the ground – Mark Waugh was one of them because of a compulsion to back the favourite in race one at Harold Park trots. Modest English off spinner Richard Dawson was poised to send down the final delivery. This was as easy as facing 'Smokey' Dawson after a day in the saddle. The half volley duly arrived and Tugga slapped it to the cover boundary to reach his century. And everyone in the ground – to a man – raised both arms above their head in celebration. The noise level was that of 40,000 rifles going off simultaneously. Tugga's Test career would proceed!

3rd Test 2005 v. Pakistan

Ricky Ponting plays the Sydney pitch even better than the great New South Welshman Michael Bevan, whom I reckon could have rattled off a Sheffield Shield ton batting with a door snake. Ponting showed his full repertoire of shots in the Australian first innings despite a head full of Wentworth Park greyhound scratchings. 'Punter' made a memorable 207 … on reaching his double century, the champion blew a kiss to his wife in the

Members Stand. His Tasmanian grade club, Mowbray, promptly sent him a stern letter fining him $20.00 for a 'public display of affection'. 'Punter' paid the fine and later admitted to fellow 'Swamp Rats' that he'd done the wrong thing. They're a hopeless bunch of romantics down there in 'Lonny'.

2nd Test 2008 v. India

Australia equalled the world record of 16 consecutive Test wins with a gut-wrenching eleventh-hour triumph. Michael Clarke pestered his captain for a bowl throughout a long, tense final afternoon ... eventually Ponting threw 'Pup' the ball. The occasional left-arm tweaker at once took three wickets in an over to win the game and went out and bought his chick an Aston Martin. 'Pup' is considering buying Fiji for Lara if he ever gets a five-wicket haul.

Anyway, I'm about to jump in my car and head to the SCG ... I'm already just a little excited.

3 January 2010

Not One Solitary Over!

On March 13, 1974, at Lancaster Park, Christchurch, New Zealand defeated Australia in an official Test match for the first time. The five wicket victory was taken around lunchtime on the fifth and final day. I was the specialist wrist spinner in the Australian team for the game ... and was not asked to bowl a single delivery in the entire match. Thank you Ian Chappell !??!

Sure, I was no Bill O'Reilly or Richie Benaud but I did have one compelling argument for being offered an over or two in this game – in my own mind, I felt I could get the crack Kiwi opener Glenn Turner out with a soggy tomato. And Turner virtually single handedly won this match for his team with 101 in the first innings and 110 not out in the second. I had victories over

Turner in county cricket, first-class cricket, one-day cricket and the First Test of the tour ... I don't know what it was ... maybe the googly hadn't made its way into New Zealand coaching manuals. Whatever it was, I regarded him as my 'bunny'. It was gutting to be denied an opportunity to undo the opposition danger man.

I had trouble getting into this game ... out for just three in the first innings, caught behind cutting at a 'nothing ball' from slow-medium pacer Bevan Congdon. These sort of bowlers always worried me ... Ian Brayshaw, the slower than slow slow-medium slow swing bowler from Western Australia only had to hand his cap to the umpire and I was a 'dead man walking'.

Back to Lancaster Park – now, of course, it has been re-named Jade Stadium – and the Kiwis are batting chasing our modest 223. Our skipper, Ian Chappell, clearly is not big fan of Turner as a man ... Chappell seems restless as the Kiwi is making few mistakes against our seam attack of Max Walker, Geoff Dymock and Greg Chappell. Turner could play this sort of bowling with a 'door snake'. I'm in the gully ... wondering when I might get a bowl ... pondering why there is so much animosity against Turner. For a start, he never comes into our dressing room at the end of the day's play for the obligatory and meaningless half hour of beer or soft drink. Chappell regards that as a debit ... I couldn't give a toss!

And then, I guess, there was that 'sin' of acknowledging one of our players with a 'Morning ... alright?' and no christian name!!! Heaven forbid!!! This was a no-no in the eyes of the 1970's Australians ... if, say, Rod Marsh on passing Turner at the pre-game nets offered 'Good morning Glenn ... how are you?' and only received 'Morning ... alright?' Marsh would feel aggrieved. Call it small minded, if you like, but it was considered a Grade One rudeness by some of our team if Christian names were not exchanged in greetings.

Anyway, back in the middle, Turner eventually falls after making his century and 74 overs have passed without me taking a turn at the bowling crease. We trail by just 32 runs but have slumped to 3–33 in our second innings with both Chappells out and New Zealand with a sniff of a kill in their nostrils. I come out to bat with the score at 1–160 late on the third day ... Dougie Walters is in great touch at the other end and the score is mounting rapidly. I'm blocking as always ... but hell, I'm in the game finally. The Hadlee brothers – Richard and Dayle – are bowling well and runs are drying up. Walters is suddenly out lbw and the tail is exposed ... I hit a couple of boundaries and remain 23 not out when Ashley Mallett edges Richard Hadlee to the 'keeper and the innings is over. As I'm walking off I start to think that, although we don't have a fat total to defend, it is the fourth innings of the match and I fancy my chances against Turner. Surely I'll get an over in the second dig.

New Zealand require 228 to beat Australia for the very first time … black blazers emerge from very dusty wardrobes all over the Canterbury province. There are five sessions remaining and a very gettable victory target. Glenn Turner is the pivot again … if he can repeat his first innings performance, the Black Caps are home. He's already getting down to business … flicking Dymock through the leg side and pushing Walker forward of point with the precision of a hand surgeon. Meanwhile, my heart is bleeding at backward point. I'd made my case the previous night to Chappell in the bar at the Avon Motor Lodge … maybe I shouldn't have had 15 beers before I'd demanded a bowl at Turner but the message had been clearly spelt out. The captain was giving me nothing … Ashley Mallett, a fine off spinner and a Chappell favourite, was in charge of the slow bowling and wasn't Turner grinning … he could pick off this variety of spin using a swizzle stick.

Turner apart, the top six batsmen in the New Zealand order had all been notches on my belt over the years. Chappell starts arguing with Turner about minding his own business at the non-strikers end … heavens above, if my leader wants to bully the eccentric Kiwi, give me a bowl!!! Fair dinkum, we're going to lose this … the crowd has swelled with the prospect of a first-ever triumph … the stands are awash with black blazers, grey trousers and beaming Bevans and misty-eyed Murrays. It's too late … five wickets have fallen … Turner is still there … he's 110 … and the target has been reached. 83.6 second innings overs delivered by our bowlers and one of the specialist spinners didn't send down any of them. We had played with 10 men!

New Zealand were worthy winners but … three years later, Australia returns to Christchurch for the first of two Tests against the locals … Greg Chappell is our skipper … I am in the team … Glen Turner captains New Zealand.

On the evening before the Test, I ask Greg to give me an early bowl against Turner. He replies, 'Any reason?' In the Lord's name, we really should have done more research on our opponents in those days. I explain that he's my 'bunny' and I'll take care of him. Greg does bring me on reasonably early in both innings of the match. Glen Turner did not dominate anywhere near as much as he had in that historic victory three years previously. In the first innings, his scoreline read: caught A Turner bowled K O'KEEFFE 15 … in the second innings, caught and bowled K O'KEEFFE 36. I rest my case!!

The Spinless Spinner

Nathan Hauritz pays a heavy price for what he is ... or isn't. I
know – it's a place I've been myself.

You see, our 'Horrie' is a spinner who doesn't spin. It's
considered cricket's mortal sin. People forget that Glen McGrath
was a fast bowler who wasn't fast and Adam Gilchrist was a
'keeper who batted better than he kept. Did those champions
have to put up with public negativity? I don't think so.

In the post-Warne era Hauritz's life is tough ... Australians are
a tough crowd. One night I expect to turn on the television and
see the off spinner in general news. There he'll be ... a prisoner in
his home with neighbours angrily waving placards out the front:
'We don't want your type around here, Hauritz!' or 'Move on,

straight breaker!' For heaven's sake, there's no shame in a 'nude nut'. Even in Hauritz's finest hour at the MCG last Wednesday there was a moment during the morning session when the Aussie slow man delivered a ball outside Mohammed Yousef's off stump. It passed Brad Haddin's gloves on the outside and raced to the boundary for four byes. Immediately, the fellow sitting next to me announced to the group, 'You think Haddin would know by now: they're not going to turn!' And everybody fell about in mocking laughter.

Within an hour, Hauritz triumphantly led his team off the ground ... a Test match winner with a five-wicket performance. This was like the plain chick winning high-school beauty queen without taking off her Coke-bottle spectacles ... this was Cinderella without the makeover.

'Horrie' had a Test 'Michelle'! (A Michelle is cricket slang for a Michelle Pfeiffer ... a 'five-fer' – get it?) There were those who thought that the only way Hauritz could have a Michelle next to his name was if he married one!

Curiously, I was told last week, Hauritz's fiancée's surname is Turner. 'He'll put an end to that before the altar,' my informant then quipped. Fair dinkum, it's relentless.

I don't care that the New South Welshman rips it less than a plastic butter knife ... there are other aspects to slow bowling, like

loop and bounce and variation of pace. These are Hauritz's strong points: in his current form he is loopier than a zany weather guy.

Bounce was his greatest asset in Melbourne and will be at the Sydney Cricket Ground this week. Balls climbing the bat accounted for four of his five Melbourne victims. The boy is bouncing … he is the flannelled equivalent of Brynne Edelstein. I was Hauritz during my playing days and I also had to wear a lot of flack. You hear the constant comments when you're on the field 'When are you going to turn one?' … or 'any chance of beating the bat, mate?' And those were just from my team-mates!

I was trusted about as much as Shane Watson in the '90s. In 1974 I played a Test against New Zealand in Christchurch as specialist spinner. The match finished late on the fifth day and I wasn't deemed good enough to be given one solitary over throughout either innings of the Kiwi victory. What was more galling was the fact that Glenn Turner scored a century in both digs to seal the win … I could bowl Turner out with a wrinkled plum! Anyway, I'm over it … just! Straight breakers deal with that sort of rejection. I salute you, Nathan Hauritz and given that in terms of thinness only the Olsen twins rival the Pakistan batting line-up, you could snare another 'Michelle' this week. Go boy!

3 January 2010

Dial M for Test Cricket

Alfred Hitchcock must have been producing the Sydney Test in recent years – all he has left out is a murder, and when Ricky Ponting won the toss on the first day and batted, some of his bowlers would not have ruled it out of the script. For three years in a row there has been intrigue, drama and an ending that nobody picked. And, thankfully, I was there for all four days again this week.

Day One

I had breakfast with Doug Walters – it's healthier to dine with Dougie at 7 am because he can't finish the meal with 'Fancy a couple of cleansing ales?'… yet! The little bloke proudly boasted that he has been off the cigarettes for exactly 'ten months and three days'. I believe he did it by laser treatment, à la *One Flew Over the Cuckoo's Nest*. I call him 'Chief'. I'm out in the middle of the SCG for ABC Radio and the pitch is greener than Bob Brown. There's so much grass Bali tourists are filling their body board covers with the loose clippings. I'm chatting to Shane Warne ... all tan and sparkling, enhanced teeth – fair dinkum, if Warney smiles near an umpire's light meter, they'll keep playing till midnight. Curator Tom Parker has prepared a pitch for the bowlers ... I wondered what he'd done since managing Elvis.

'Punter' bats! It's a brave move given that our batsmen would have problems with swing listening to a Glenn Miller album. As usual, Phil Hughes is throwing the kitchen sink at everything ... unfortunately, however, he's batting in the lounge room. Michael Bevan would be the best batting coach for Hughes – they share similar footwork and scoring zones and 'Bevo' did all right after he figured out what worked at the top level. Out in the middle, Mohammed Asif does a Glen McGrath on us and we're all out for a total akin to an NBL crowd. My horse, Skulla's Sister, wins a three-horse 1100-metre sprint at Gilgandra in the late afternoon and pays $1.40 ... my only query now is can she get the 2000 metres of the Cox Plate?

Day Two

Pakistan should press their advantage today as the clouds have lifted. Their coach, Intikhab Alam, is chatting to his players in the nets – I played against 'Inti' and saw him as a father figure then … in 1971! Before play, I'm having coffee with some bushies in the members area. Doug Walters rings and says he's outside and does not have an entry ticket. A young turnstile operator has asked him to prove he's Doug Walters by smoking. 'I don't smoke!' he's said. 'Well, if you don't smoke, you're not Doug Walters!' the young 'un argues. If he'd only produced a can of beer to prove identification, Dougy would have been in within minutes. Kevin Rudd walks past … apparently the PM was a wicket-keeper for Nambour Thirds. He should be mentoring Kamran Akmal!

A statue of Stan McCabe is unveiled … Bradman reckoned 'Napper' McCabe played the best innings ever during a 1938 Test against England. 'Napper' was a product of St Joseph's College, Hunters Hill, where legendary coach Tony Lantry has been the cricket master for a very long time. Tony reportedly identified 'Napper' as having potential when he joined the senior school in 1919 … just kidding, Tony! Australia bowls well as a group and Pakistan waste a golden opportunity to lead by 350 … the lead in the end is 206. The door is ajar!

Day Three

It's Jane McGrath Day and we're all in pink. Every bloke in the ground looks like he is auditioning to play Mr Humphries in *Are You Being Served?* Sydney is at its best when supporting worthy causes.

Shane Watson is batting brilliantly – he looks so well set – he's a special for 90-odd! 'Punter' gets out cheaply again … Mike Brearley has texted him: 'You're so me at the moment – short of runs but leading well.' The ball is reverse swinging and Danish Kaneria is bowling like Anil Kumble. Wickets fall regularly on a grey afternoon. Only Mike Hussey stands up … under pressure yet again, 'Mr Cricket' must at times feel like he's on death row waiting for the Governor to grant him a pardon. His crisp and calculated batting has given him a stay of execution. Marcus North, on the other hand, continues to play down the Illawarra line … when he should be on the East Hills. At stumps Pakistan are on the brink of victory … Australia lead by 80 with only two wickets remaining.

Day Four

From the opening delivery, Mohammed Yousuf ordered a centre wicket practice session for the Australian batsmen … 'just play yourself in boys, we'll hang around the boundaries and throw the ball back'. Yousuf was to talk later of not dealing with the pressure … how about applying it occasionally. Eventually Australia is dismissed and Pakistan need 176 to win. Plenty of time, but, hey, let's treat it like a 50-over game. Yes … bowled out in 38 overs … 36 runs short. Many congratulations to Australia for a miracle win. The admirable Nathan Hauritz snares another 'Michelle' – five wickets with well-disguised off spinners … so well disguised they didn't look like off spinners. 'Horry' is David Copperfield … a master of illusion. Long may his magical powers continue to grow. A victorious Ponting explains that his game plan was for his team to score more in the first innings than the Pakistanis in the fourth innings. Close but no cigar for that either, 'Punter'. I know varieties of cucumber that could have batted more intelligently and caught better than Pakistan … if they'd done either marginally better the visitors would have won by an innings.

10 January 2010

Choc Behind the Wheel

Two words – Anthony Mundine!! That should be enough to grab the attention of a few more readers. Now I can continue.

Has there been an Australian sportsman who has polarised red-blooded opinion more than the great 'Choc'? No sooner had he chalked up another victory over 'Deadly' Rob Medley last Monday than 150 comments were posted on this newspaper's review of the fight. A great majority were negative.

I don't know 'Choc' very well but from my limited experiences with him I like the fellow a great deal … and what an athlete! His unique psyche – which makes Warney look as retiring as Howard Hughes – plus his wide range of skills would make him a great wrist spinner … in fact, could someone involved in the Cricket

Australia coaching set-up teach him the rudiments of leg spin, give him ten months of concentrated practice and launch him on the Poms next December? Traditionally stars obliterate English cricketers ... and 'Choc' is undoubtedly a star! With Mundine's leggies and self-belief, the Aussie attack would regain the Ashes for sure. The disappointments of missing an NRL premiership will seem small potatoes alongside an Ashes triumph.

I spent a week with Mundine at the Celebrity Grand Prix in Melbourne a few years ago – I finished 23rd out of 25, beating two super models who I reckon were doing their nails during five laps of the race. 'Choc' drove like a demon for a close fourth behind 'Awesome Foursome' rower James Tomkins.

During the five days prior to the event we travelled as a group by bus to Sandown racetrack to work on our driving skills. My fellow 'celebrities' included mostly Victorian comedians, radio personalities, former politicians, sportsmen and models. None had previously met Mundine and only judged him on unpopular opinions.

On the first morning, they kept a seat for me at the front of the bus with the ringing endorsement, 'Stay up here with us, Skull ... let that bighead Mundine sit down the back.' Knowing the real Mundine, I said: 'By the fourth day, you'll have been charmed by "Choc" and I'll be back with the baggage.' On only the third day, I was late onto the bus and there they were, all over Mundine like cheap suits. Someone ushered me past with a 'There's plenty of room at the back, Skull … tell us another one, Choccy.' Fair dinkum, life can be fickle!

◈

If Stuart MacGill had been granted one wish, he'd have opened the batting at Bellerive Oval. Of course, dear Stuey wouldn't have got any runs, but it's a bit like a date with Paris Hilton – you still fancy your chances!

The Hobart pitch is made of rye … pop ham and tomato on it and it's a great sandwich but bowlers don't find it all that palatable.

Ricky Ponting should have made a duck on Thursday when a sitter was dropped at fine leg. Fair dinkum, the Pakistanis must immediately draft Winona Ryder into their squad – she's always been good with her hands. Mike Hussey managed only six. It's back on the tightrope for 'Mr Cricket', who must feel like a weather forecaster – people take it for granted when he gets it right but when he gets it wrong they chorus, 'How does he stay in the job?'

Ponting is batting with his vice-captain, Michael Clarke, and runs are coming at a remarkable rate. Milestones are reached.

'Pup' is all over 'Punter' in the Matt Hayden/Justin Langer groping style. 'Punter', on the other hand, is all quick handshake and let's get on with the business. On reaching his ton, 'Pup' is up for a Burt Lancaster-like roll on the beach ... 'Punter' offers his hand as if he was thanking a fourth umpire at the end of the match. Ponting makes Harry Callaghan look sentimental.

Cricket tragic Kevin Rudd is in the Australian dressing room at stumps asking to bat before the declaration tomorrow. The Aussies can expect to see a lot of Tony Abbott in his baggy green budgie smugglers if there is a change of government next election.

Just before stumps, Kamran Akmal is contemplating a streak across the ground. The wicket-keeper reckons if he catches the attention of security guards at least he's caught something this series. Out in the middle, 'Punter' reaches his double century and there are more handshakes with 'Pup'. Doesn't anybody hug any more?

Marcus North is batting ... not for long enough, however. Is he the perfect fit at number six? Maybe he hasn't got the powers of acceleration to fully suit that role. It is like playing Carl Webb on the wing. Shaun Marsh – a player with so many extra dimensions to his game – is at hand. His challenge very soon will be to keep his younger brother Mitchell at bay.

Our prime minister is at the ground again, bowling leg spinners to children ... I've seen better actions in the Court of Petty Sessions.

Finally it's stumps on the second day and Australia is in a dominant position – Pakistani opener Salman Butt has comically run out two of his partners, including his captain. Walking off the ground, Butt requested security to stay with him inside the dressing room.

17 January 2010

Ashes Memories

I'm at the Brit Oval on the morning of day four of the fifth Ashes Test. The Poms have set Australia 546 to retain the Ashes and by stumps the previous evening we had reached 80 without loss.

It's a game the selectors have cocked up. We left out the specialist spinner on a pitch drier than Jack Benny. Playing the extra fast bowler instead of Nathan Hauritz was the equivalent of readying yourself for a day on Bondi beach by packing a dinner suit.

I'm ringside amongst 80-odd optimistic Australians who believe we may still do it. Most of us are drinking Pimms; the home supporters are drinking tea and coffee and deep down they feel those pesky Australians may just get there. It's the English way. Two wickets fall early … at once the English are now drinking Pimms … then come Ricky Ponting and Mike Hussey with a long and dangerous partnership. The English are back on the coffee and watching every ball uncomfortably. Each Aussie boundary is greeted with an eerie silence. 'Say it isn't so, Straussy', their faces lament.

Then it happens. At 2–217 and with double centuries beckoning for Punter and Mr Cricket, a risky single to Andrew Flintoff has been taken. 'Freddy', whose leg injury is so bad that Stuart Broad would have preferred Captain Ahab as his mid-on, has picked the ball up and thrown down the stumps with Punter appearing short of his ground. Thirteen thousand Englishmen go ballistic but the decision has been referred upstairs. The buzz … the expectation … the nervousness … and finally, the OUT. London explodes.

Thirty-nine overs later the Ashes are gone. *Land of Hope and Glory* has been sung for the four-thousandth time. All I want to do is drink my Pimms in peace and sundry Poms are slapping me on the back with shouts of 'Unlucky, dingo' and 'Tough luck, Skippy'. As in 2005 we've been broken at The Oval. Let's not play there in 2013.

23 August 2009

My Pursuit of a Television Set

It was mid summer in northern England. I was in the heart of the cotton city of Blackburn playing Lancashire League cricket as the overseas professional for East Lancashire and enjoying a rather good season. I was the fittest I'd ever been, having linked with a marathon runner called Dave Walsh and embarking on gruelling 15 kilometre runs three or four times a week around the outskirts of this sprawling town. I'd shed about 10 kilos in weight and was in peak condition every weekend for East Lancashire.

An invitation had come to play in a match for Derek Robins against the Yorkshire County team. I'd played for Derek Robins a few years previously and enjoyed the occasion. His matches are very competitive and although not regarded as first class fixtures there is an edge to the encounters. Traditionally Derek assembles a team who will enjoy each other's company and can play a little bit as well.

I drove to Harrogate on the morning of the game. It's a small English village in west Yorkshire. The summer of '75 had been relatively dry and the pitch looked quite bare as I entered the ground. I was to be in good hands over the next few days as Brian Close, my former Somerset captain, was to lead us and I knew two or three of the others in my team, notably Ian Botham, Geoff Howarth, Geoff Miller and Graham Roope. The match began … we won the toss and batted … a good move.

I am a bit of a television fanatic but this summer I had a problem. I was staying at the Blackburn YMCA during my stint with East Lancs. I had a single bedroom apartment. You could only squeeze a bed and a basin in it … there was no toilet and the showers were communal. The only television set at the Y was downstairs next to the dining room.

My fellow YMCA lodgers were students mainly from all over Europe and Africa. There were Swedes, Finns, Greeks, Nigerians and Kenyans. It was a great mix and we all got on well though very few of them could talk much English and none knew about cricket. I liked eating with them at meal times but could never get near the television set as they watched endless documentaries on BBC2. Most of my weekday nights were spent in my room reading

or writing letters back home. I yearned for my own television set
… a simple portable would have done that I could prop up in my
room and watch to my heart's content. How could I get one? I was
an impoverished professional cricketer staying at a hostel … the
price of a portable television set was beyond me.

As luck would have it the man of the match for Yorkshire v.
D H Robins XI was to receive a brand new £150 portable television
set with antenna. I saw it on the trophy cabinet as I walked into the
Robins dressing room … I would kill for that television set … but
cricket is a team game so I could not let my selfish ambitions be
too naked. Our opening batsmen were Howarth of New Zealand
and Jimmy Love of Yorkshire. They prospered against what was
a weakened Yorkshire attack and, rather fortunately, the great
Geoffrey Boycott wasn't playing … that was a plus for everybody.

Howarth and Love went along swimmingly on a benign pitch
… Love made 95 before being stumped off Phil Carrick, a left arm
orthodox spinner who was turning the ball despite not enjoying
a reputation as a legitimate tweaker … good signs for me and the
television set. Clive Rice of South Africa was in next … he was
an all rounder who would have played tremendous test cricket at
his peak yet because of their international ban was condemned to
display his professional skills in England and elsewhere. Batting at
three he looked in tremendous form, holding the bat upright and

slapping anything overpitched through extra cover. Eventually he was bowled by Arnold Sidebottom for 63.

Close failed – out for four caught slogging one up in the air off Carrick. Roope came in and in partnership with Ian Botham our total was rattling along. Roope was one of the best catchers I've ever seen throughout my career and was a real spring-heeled jack in the slip cordon – his years of goal keeping for Corinthian Casuals had sharpened his reflexes. Perhaps he should have played more tests but he and a youthful Botham who made 40 were giving our momentum a real boost.

I was listed to bat at number seven and I was in with the total on 283. 'Roopey' and I were in partnership and I was enjoying myself. My batting had come a long way through my fitness levels being so high and I was working the ball through extra cover, whipping it off my pads ... I felt comfortable ... there was nobody really quick in the opposition. Sidebottom was honest, Carrick was accurate, and Geoff Cope – a seasoned bespectacled off spinner whose right elbow at release made Murali's arm look fused – was operating and giving me width ... I was slapping him through point. I had a polyarmour bat which was just a cannon ... I loved this bat ... I slept with this bat. When you haven't got a television in your room you need a good bat! At times in my room at the YMCA I would just clean that bat ... it stood next to the bed and often I'd just wake up and play a shot with it. Every time I looked to punch the ball I found a gap and the boundary. Eventually when Closey declared we had a total of 404 for 8 down and I was 65 not out. Okay that's at least the antenna of my television set.

Yorkshire were batting on the second day and the late Barry 'Bart' Stead was bowling well. Bart was a left arm seamer who bent the ball back in ... he looked 60 when he was 20 and he died young. Bart was never here for a long time ... he was here for a good time. He could have smoked for England and drunk for Great Britain. He was such a character! This day he removed both openers cheaply.

Clive Rice bowled a few overs but on this sluggish surface there was nothing much in it for Ricey ... I'm pleased with that because after his first innings of 63 he was an early contender for man of the match.

Miller was bowling off spin and not looking too threatening. Closey has thrown me the ball ... at once I'm turning it rather a long way ... this was a pitch I wanted to take all around the world. The Yorkies have never had a history of playing leg spin well and I am inducing leading edges to cover, bowling people through the gate and eventually getting them to chip back to me looking to work through the leg side.

In between times Carrick is hitting me for boundaries as is Peter Squires who had come in at number three and did well for 64. This ground is lightning fast and whenever I erred in length or line I paid with a boundary. Nonetheless a return of 5–86 off 20 overs is worthy of leading the team off the field. I'm ahead in the man of the match reckoning. Love, Roope and Rice are in a pack behind me.

We're batting again. Rice and Love are already into the 20s but Closey declares before either of them has a chance to play a significant innings. I don't bat in the second dig.

The Yorkshiremen are set 359 odd to win on the last day. The pitch is already showing signs of wear … Carrick and Cope have turned prodigiously.

After multiple scotches prior to the final day, Closey says to me, 'Kerry you bowl that funny stuff … I'm going to give you a long bowl on the last day – don't let me down lad.' No problems captain! I've got one hand on the television set. A match-winning innings from a Yorkshireman and I'm dead, however, and it would be in my interests if Rice, Botham or Roope don't take too many wickets. Isn't cricket selfish on occasions??

On the final morning I have problems. Barrie Leadbeater is crunching boundaries off everybody including myself. I'm in trouble … Leadbeater is going to get Yorkshire across the line here and I'm going to have to watch documentaries in the common room for the rest of my stay in Blackburn. My spinning finger is bleeding courtesy of those twenty overs in the first innings ... I'm impervious to pain though at this stage ... it's all about the television set.

Almost at once Sidebottom chips one straight back to me for a caught and bowled ... Carrick goes for a cow shot and loses middle stump ... Roope at slip holds Graham 'Moonbeam' Stevenson and I have three wickets ... Rice has come on and got two from the other end ... damn it – bugger those South Africans. If he gets five I'm dead! ...

There's three to go. It will serve me best if Bart comes back and he duly does so and on cue gets a wicket. There's just two left ... there's blood all over my fingers ... Rice keeps asking the captain bring him on again ... he wants that TV set as well. Stuff him, bloody South Africans they're always after the booty. Closey looks at my hand ... 'OK lad you've got three wickets I'll just let the quicks clean up.' 'No Brian, please, it's okay,' I plead. 'But there's blood on the ball, lad,' he says. 'I don't care, I'll rip these last two out for you,' I declare. I'm into my 24th over. I'm tired. Apart from the bleeding finger I've been on the drink the previous night with Botham, Howarth and Bart ... I'm dehydrated ... I can hardly walk. There's two wickets available ...

we're going to win ... Leadbeater is out for 110 ... it's a century in a losing team ... I've got eight wickets in the match so far on top of my runs ... I've almost got that set. Closey keeps me on ... I'm wiping blood off the ball with a towel ... I'm bowling dross ... Cope, although wicketless during the game, is slogging me ... this bespectacled twig of a man is raining on my parade and keeps hitting me for six. Closey has signalled for Rice to warm up ... he already has two wickets ... if he gets four for the innings I'm dead! Suddenly Howard Cooper goes for a big swing and nicks my leg break to slip and Love catches a blinder – I've got four – one to go.

By this stage I've got no skin on my index or middle finger at all ... the ball is resting against raw bone. Yorkshire still need another 100 and Cope is 32 not out. He's trying to get them over the line. He launches into another cow shot ... Bart is at deep mid wicket ... the worst catcher in the team and he's been on the whisky till 5 am ... I'm thinking that he's going to palm this for six, Closey's going to take me off and Rice will get the last wicket and the television set. Bart has lunged to his right ... the ball has struck him on the wrist, then the mouth and as he's tumbled it's fallen into his considerable midriff where he grasps it with both hands. The match is over. I have 5–76. The Robbins XI has won by 90 runs ... now for the presentations.

Everybody is shaking my hand and I'm apologising for the blood. I'm standing there cradling a can of Yorkshire bitter beer. The captains are thanked and presented with gifts for competing and it's time now for the man of the match. There's some shuffling ... will Leadbeater get it ... there are a lot of Yorkshiremen on the presentation dais ... will Rice get the sympathy vote for being South African ... Robins is a known South African sympathiser. All sorts of thoughts are racing through my head. Roopey fielded like a genius and bludgeoned 78 in the first innings ... Love got 98 and 24 to set up the run chase ... another Yorkshireman ... am I going to fall victim to the Yorkshire bias. I've got three more months in the country – I can't possibly watch one more documentary. The President of Yorkshire then announces: 'And the Man of the Match please give him a round of applause from' ... please say Australia, please say Australia ... 'from Australia Kerry O'Keeffe.' Yes!!! Thank you!!! And he lifts the television set and presents it to me and I stagger off to put it in the car and then return to celebrate with my team-mates over another copious amount of Yorkshire bitter.

I've got my television set. I drive back to the YMCA ... its after midnight ... the night watchman lets me in ... he thinks I've pinched what's under my arm ... I race up to my room and assemble it ... put up the antenna ... switch it on and yes there's a documentary but I don't care … it's my television set. I can change channels without seeking approval from anybody.

Thank you Derek Robins. Thank you Yorkshire for not being able to play leg breaks. Thank you Brian Close for disregarding the blood on the ball and keeping me on. I enjoyed the last three months at the YMCA despite shared showers, crap food and an inability to discuss any cricket at the dining room table – I had my TV.

Yorkshire v DH Robins' XI

DH Robins' XI first innings		Runs	Balls	Mins	4s	6s
GP Howarth	c Bottomley b Sidebottom	35				
JD Love	st Bottomley b Carrick	95				
CEB Rice	b Sidebottom	63				
*DB Close	c Leadbeater b Carrick	4				
GRJ Roope	b Robinson	78				
IT Botham	c Leadbeater b Carrick	40				
KJ O'Keeffe	not out	65				
DJ Brickett	b Robinson	1				
G Miller	run out	5				
+A Long	not out	5				
B Stead	did not bat					
Extras		13				
Total (8 wickets, declared, 100 overs)		404				

Fall of wickets: 1-88, 2-201, 3-201, 4-217, 5-283, 6-346, 7-348, 8-365

Yorkshire bowling	Overs	Mdns	Runs	Wkts	Wides	No-Balls
Robinson	20	1	86	2	-	2
Cooper	16	3	62	0	-	1
Sidebottom	19	4	43	2	-	-
Carrick	25	2	91	3	-	-
Townsley	6	2	19	0	-	1
Cope	14	1	90	0	-	-

Yorkshire first innings		Runs	Balls	Mins	4s	6s
B Leadbeater	b Stead	43				
RAJ Townsley	c Brickett b Stead	6				
PJ Squires	c Close b O'Keeffe	64				
A Sidebottom	run out	24				
GB Stevenson	c Brickett b O'Keeffe	16				
P Carrick	c Brickett b O'Keeffe	50				
*JH Hampshire	c Roope b Close	7				
HP Cooper	b O'Keeffe	1				
GA Cope	c and b Stead	0				
AL Robinson	c and b O'Keeffe	14				
+SM Bottomley	not out	0				
Extras		13				
Total (all out, 75.1 overs)		238				

Fall of wickets: 1-14, 2-105, 3-124, 4-148, 5-168, 6-177, 7-193, 8-194, 9-213, 10-238 (75.1 ov)

DH Robins' XI bowling	Overs	Mdns	Runs	Wkts	Wides	No-Balls
Stead	16	5	38	3	-	-
Brickett	10	5	12	0	-	4
Rice	9	3	22	0	-	1
Miller	12	3	43	0	-	-
O'Keeffe	20.1	7	86	5	-	-
Botham	4	0	5	0	-	-
Close	4	1	19	1	-	-

DH Robins' XI second innings		Runs	Balls	Mins	4s	6s
GP Howarth	c Bottomley b Sidebottom	24				
JD Love	c and b Carrick	24				
CEB Rice	c Bottomley b Carrick	27				
GRJ Roope	not out	37				
IT Botham	not out	33				
G Miller	b Townsley	15				
*DB Close	did not bat					
KJ O'Keeffe	did not bat					
DJ Brickett	did not bat					
+A Long	did not bat					
B Stead	did not bat					
Extras		8				
Total (4 wickets, declared, 51.1 overs)		168				
Fall of wickets: 1-35, 2-52, 3-91, 4-97						

Yorkshire bowling	Overs	Mdns	Runs	Wkts	Wides	No-Balls
Robinson	5	3	10	0	-	-
Stevenson	1	0	4	0	-	-
Sidebottom	9	1	28	1	-	-
Cooper	9	4	11	0	-	-
Carrick	13	1	46	2	-	-
Cope	4.1	0	13	0	-	-
Townsley	10	1	48	1	-	2

Yorkshire second innings		Runs	Balls	Mins	4s	6s
B Leadbeater	c Long b Rice	110				
RAJ Townsley	c Long b Rice	16				
PJ Squires	c and b Roope	12				
A Sidebottom	c and b O'Keeffe	13				
GB Stevenson	c Roope b O'Keeffe	1				
P Carrick	b O'Keeffe	6				
*JH Hampshire	c Howarth b Stead	8				
HP Cooper	c Love b O'Keeffe	6				
GA Cope	c Stead b O'Keeffe	32				
AL Robinson	not out	14				
+SM Bottomley	run out	0				
Extras		26				
Total (all out, 83.4 overs)		244				

Fall of wickets: 1-41, 2-74, 3-109, 4-123, 5-128, 6-138, 7-154, 8-226, 9-230, 10-244 (83.4 ov)

DH Robins' XI bowling	Overs	Mdns	Runs	Wkts	Wides	No-Balls
Stead	15	5	19	1	-	-
Brickett	6	1	14	0	4	3
O'Keeffe	26.4	4	76	5	1	1
Botham	2	1	4	0	1	-
Rice	11	7	18	2	-	-
Roope	9	2	16	1	-	-
Miller	5	0	29	0	-	-
Close	9	1	42	0	-	-

2, 3, 4 July 1975

The Twitter
Winter of 2010

My off-season stretches from the Golden Slipper sprint in early
April to the start of finals footy in September. I purposely do not
know how to use Twitter and have avoided the urge to initiate a
Facebook site, and since I can't or won't do Sudoku to keep the
mind sharp I have taken to writing a diary: it's my private form
of Twitter … a collection of tweets and Facebook entries. If I did
both, these would be some of my contributions.

❖

On 3 April, Crystal Lily won this year's Slipper and jockey Brett
Prebble said, 'She's going to be a super three-year-old.' Prebble is a

believable judge – I'm going to back this girl throughout her next campaign.

◈

The Chennai Super Kings won the IPL Twenty20 with Doug Bollinger central to the triumph. Whenever the talented left-arm paceman does any media appearance or interviews it is only on the proviso that there be no mention of his hairpiece ... anyway, 'Doug the Rug' took 12 wickets in eight games in a superb display of producing under pressure – the yorkers, bumpers and slower balls were cleverly concocted and the former Seven Hills RSL first-change trundler was awarded 'Hair' – I mean 'Mayor' – of Chennai' status.

◈

Early May is Logie night and Ray 'Megsy' Meagher won the Gold Logie after 22 years of 'stone the flamin' crows' as Alf Stewart. Meagher is popular on and off the set of *Home and Away* and those who played club rugby union with him in Brisbane reckon he's a 'bonzer bloke'. Onya, 'Megsy'! *Packed to the Rafters* was voted Most Popular Drama Series ... my wife never misses an episode. I would rather watch hour after hour of Geoff Marsh endlessly working the ball to third man for singles than watch this serial. Fair dinkum, could the writers maybe introduce the odd murder or even a smidgen of gratuitous violence ... or maybe Rebecca 'Goody Two Shoes' Gibney could say 'shit' or something as head-turning. The plot of the mind-numbing *Bold and the Beautiful* looks to be hyperactive by comparison.

◆

Australia is beaten by England in the final of Twenty20 World Cup ... the Poms slaughtered our back-up bowlers, whose eight overs cost 86 runs. Michael Clarke, destined to be an outstanding Test batsman, appears as comfortable in this form of the game as Fuifui Moimoi would be in high beam gymnastics. Dirk Nannes, an alpine skier who reportedly is not particularly fond of cricket, led the tournament's leading wicket-takers – Dirk could be anything if he actually starts to like the game.

◆

By mid-winter Queensland had beaten New South Wales 3–0 again in the State of Origin Rugby League series … and well done to a fabulous squad of footballers. And, look, I'm as true blue New South Wales as they come, but the result is disappointing … nothing graver. Very few south of the Tweed are googling 'self-harm kits'. Sure, we are accused of lacking the necessary passion for this type of competition – mate against mate, and all that. Personally, I simply do not get the overly hyped marketing of the contests. If Test Rugby League was more competitive I would salivate over the Kangaroos, but sadly a nation like France is a shadow of its 1951 self. (Yes, I'm a dinosaur!) And, to boot, it's unbalanced for the Cane Toads up north to put winning a footy match between neighbouring states as a priority to sit alongside breathing and eating. Most of us Cockroaches just couldn't care: we have Sydney Harbour and 400 State rugby league titles still won't get you that wonder of the world! LOL!

Ricky Ponting has drawn a Test series one-all in England against Pakistan. Australia has won only three Tests out of 12 on English pitches under his captaincy … the possibility of 'Punter' returning for the 2013 Ashes campaign aged 38 must now be negligible.

England, under the coaching of the much-admired tough-nut Andy Flower, are now difficult to beat. Flower, incidentally, averaged 53.70 as a batsman/wicketkeeper in 55 Tests for Zimbabwe: a better return even than that of the 47.60 of the genius Adam Gilchrist.

❖

It's a cold August evening and I have just watched video footage of the great W. G. Grace ... he once made 400 not out against 22 fielders and was still opening in Tests for England at the age of 56! Even Mike 'Mr Cricket' Hussey might be retired by that age ... or maybe not.

❖

The Wallabies just cannot beat the All Blacks in Rugby tests ... Graham Henry's team have simply worked out how to beat Australia. A Maori friend of mine reckons our coach Robbie Deans is a double agent. Bollocks, even New Zealanders wouldn't try something like that.

❖

Word out of the England cricket camp is that they now believe they can retain the Ashes this summer. This followed hot on the heels of the news that cricketing maverick Greg Chappell has been named as a full-time national selector. Regardless, Australia should still take the series. England will potentially have two, maybe three, days of humid overcast conditions during the series; James Anderson and company will need to take 10 Australian wickets on each of those days to be in the contest. I'm backing the Croatian–Australian Simon Katich to get 500-plus runs in a man of the series summer. 'Kat's' exaggerated footwork to cover his off stump against the moving ball is foolproof. Gun wicket-taker Mitchell Johnson's erratic method is best suited to the hard pitches of Australia and South Africa ... if I was an Australian selector, I would not take him on tour north of the Tropic of Capricorn.

❖

Sir Garfield Sobers was the best cricketer of my era – I reckon, any era. I read today that the great West Indian left-hander was born with six fingers on each hand. 'The first extra finger fell off quite early, when I was 9 or 10 ... I took the second off when I was 14 or 15,' he claims. Wow! Lucky for him the others stayed on!

◈

I've enjoyed this tweeting … maybe Facebook is an option.